ADVICE ON ESTABLISHING A LIBRARY

Composuisse libros, promptum et cuique est triviale;
Librorum auctores composuisse, tuum est.

ADVICE ON ESTABLISHING A LIBRARY

By Gabriel Naudé

With an Introduction by Archer Taylor

Berkeley and Los Angeles

UNIVERSITY OF CALIFORNIA PRESS

1950

UNIVERSITY OF CALIFORNIA PRESS
BERKELEY AND LOS ANGELES
CALIFORNIA

◇

CAMBRIDGE UNIVERSITY PRESS
LONDON, ENGLAND

COPYRIGHT, 1950, BY
THE REGENTS OF THE UNIVERSITY OF CALIFORNIA

Contents

Introduction, by Archer Taylor	vii
Notice to the Reader	xvii
Naudé's Address to His Patron	1
Why Establish a Library?	5
Preparing for the Task	10
The Number of Books	14
Selecting the Books	20
Procuring the Books	47
The Building and Its Location	59
Arranging the Books	63
Ornament and Decoration	70
The Purpose of a Library	74
Notes to the Present Edition	83
References	103
Index of Persons	105

Introduction

THE ERUDITE AND *industrious Gabriel Naudé (1600–1653) was one of the first to make librarianship a career. Before his day, men had made systematic purchases of books for their own collections or those of others, had managed libraries, compiled bibliographies, or performed other tasks now done by librarians; but these occupations had been only incidental to the daily demands of a monastic order, the instruction of a monarch or some member of a great family, or to other work that was considered more important. Naudé, however, early became associated with a large private library, and when he found himself unable to pursue his chosen profession he devoted his energies entirely to libraries.*

As a young man, Naudé undertook the study of medicine under the professor and bibliophile René Moreau. When Moreau's death interrupted his studies, he found a patron in Henri de Mesme, Councilor of State, who commissioned him to manage and enlarge his library. Naudé took the work seriously; with zeal and skill, he made the Bibliotheca Memmiana famous in the early seventeenth century.

Naudé, desiring to return to his medical studies, obtained leave from De Mesme to study at Padua, but his stay there was cut short by his father's death. On his return to Paris he undertook to copy Pierre Charron's correspondence—the manuscript is still in existence—and by this means confirmed his admiration of that great skeptic and rationalist. In 1631 he went to Rome with Pierre du Puy, librarian of the De Thou collection, which, though small at that time, was to become one of the great libraries of the century. He stayed in Rome twelve years, finding employment in one or another of the large private libraries of that city. At different times he was librarian to two cardinals, the bibliophiles De Bagni and Barberini.

In 1642, Cardinal Richelieu recalled him to Paris to be the librarian of his personal collection. Soon after Naudé arrived, Richelieu died, and he was employed by Cardinal Mazarin instead. Without delay he set out to create a great library. Some complained that his journeys, which took him as far as Flanders, England, and Italy, prevented his attending fully to his duties; but it was generally recognized that he was a competent and successful administrator. It was at his suggestion that Cardinal Mazarin opened his library to the public at regularly appointed hours.

In the course of his duties Naudé compiled a catalogue of Canon Descordes's library (1643). This was

INTRODUCTION

being offered for sale en bloc, *and in order to appraise its value Naudé made a catalogue according to subjects, the first catalogue of a private library to find general use as a reference book and therefore a landmark in the history of libraries.*

As a consequence of political disputes Mazarin's collections were scattered. Naudé was sorely distressed; he salvaged what he could at the public sale, and later he took part in the rebuilding of the library, which survives as the Bibliothèque Mazarine.

In 1652, Queen Christina called him to Sweden as librarian to succeed Vossius. Christina had assembled a group of brilliant Frenchmen in Upsala, but Naudé did not find the Swedish court congenial and returned to France the following year. He died at Abbeville on his way back to Paris.

The bibliography of Naudé's published works is long. Besides medical papers, his early works include an attack on the Rosicrucians (1623), who curiously mingled charlatanry, philosophy, and science. His interests in such bypaths found a fuller expression in his first famous book, the Apologie pour tous les grands personnages qui ont été faussement soupçonnés de magie *(1635), a rationalist's defense of such men as Pythagoras, Roger Bacon, and Cornelius Agrippa. He also wrote history, biography, and a defense of Mazarin. Most of his works include an abundance of bibliographical detail; his interest in books and libraries was his paramount concern throughout his life.*

Avis pour dresser une bibliothèque *was one of his early works; it first appeared in 1627. It was the only one of Naudé's books that went into a second edition, which was published in 1644. John Evelyn, the diarist, published an English translation,* Instructions concerning Erecting of a Library, *in 1661.*

Naudé's Advice *is one of the earliest works on librarianship. It begins with a defense of collecting books and includes an account of books to be bought and books to be passed by, a discussion of schemes for arranging a library, and a description of a proper library building and its ornaments. His recommendations concerning the purchase of books are especially interesting. They do not follow in all respects the practice of modern librarians. Standard works and the best authors are of course recommended; so also are reference works. Besides these obvious categories, which no one would question, Naudé urges the purchase of the earliest treatises on special subjects because they are usually better than later works. Perhaps inspired by his interest in magic and the Rosicrucians, he recommends buying books on out-of-the-way subjects.*

To the modern reader perhaps the most impressive parts of the book are those which show Naudé's liberal and open mind. He insists that a library should con-

INTRODUCTION

tain books on both sides of important questions. His own writings show his interest in science, and yet he recommends the purchase of books written against science. He recommends also the books of the "Novators," the men who were writing against orthodox Aristotelian philosophy. This attitude is most clearly shown in his suggesting—although he was a good churchman and was to be closely associated all his life with some of the most important prelates of his time—that heretical works should have a place.

The seventh chapter deals with the arrangement of books in a library. Naudé rejected certain arrangements then in use, such as classifying them all arbitrarily under the three headings: Morals, Sciences, and Devotion; he chose rather what is virtually the modern classification by subjects. He found some difficulty with books that treated several subjects, but thought them too few to cause serious annoyance. He condemned the entirely unclassified arrangement of the Ambrosian Library because it required catalogues of both authors and subjects. Like modern librarians, he kept manuscripts apart from books.

Although the Advice *was reprinted, it does not appear to have circulated widely in its day. The Latin translation of it, which was included in an omnibus volume of treatises on libraries compiled in the latter years of the seventeenth century, was the most im-*

portant and effective recognition of its value. Evelyn's translation was printed in a small edition only, and this contained many printer's errors. Evelyn was so displeased that he endeavored to buy up and destroy the copies that had passed into circulation. Thus the English version was never widely distributed.

With the exception of a few bibliophile's editions within the last century, neither the French original nor the English translation has been easily available to the modern reader. Yet the Advice *is an important book in the history of learning. Although Naudé did not strive to be encyclopedic and apparently jotted down as illustrative examples only those titles and authors that came to mind as he wrote, he nevertheless presented a survey of contemporary scholarship. He suggested many of the principles that now govern library practice: the importance of preserving and consulting the records of past ages (Naudé urged the purchase of translations for the benefit of the unlearned), the careful supervision of the lending of books, the convenient classification and arrangement of a library, and the granting of free access to it at appointed hours. Evelyn correctly estimated the merit of the* Advice *by inscribing a presentation copy of his translation with the words: "It is yet a very useful discourse."*

It had been the original intention to reprint Evelyn's translation about as it stood, with due attention to the "printer's errors" mentioned above. But it became obvious in the work of preparation for the press that there were numerous errors which could not possibly be worked off so easily on the usual whipping post of authors, and the version now offered, in which Mr. W. H. Alexander, Mr. John S. Gildersleeve, Mr. Harold A. Small, and Mr. Thompson Webb, Jr., have collaborated at sundry times and in diverse manners, is substantially independent, and, salva reverentia, *improved. But when Evelyn hit upon a happy phrase, his language has been retained.*

ARCHER TAYLOR

Advice on Establishing a Library

TO THE READER

THESE COUNSELS having taken shape only through a chance argument pursued some months since in the library of one who did me the favor then and there of treating them as entertaining, I had never dreamed of wiping the dust of my study off them, to expose them to the light of day; but finally, not being able more effectively or promptly to satisfy the curiosity of many of my friends who were asking for copies, I made up my mind to do so, as much to free myself from the expense of hiring copyists and the inconvenience of having them around as from being naturally inclined to oblige the public at large. Should these counsels fail, as unworthy to satisfy that public, at least they could serve as guide to those who would provide it with better, in order that men may no longer remain deprived of a work which seems wanting to their felicity and out of respect for which I have forced myself to be first to break the ice and trace hurriedly the route for those who would like to pursue it again more at their leisure. If you are grateful to me for this, I shall have reason to esteem your good-will and courteous consideration. If not, I shall entreat you to be willing at least to excuse my faults and—the Printer's.

Advice on Establishing a Library
PRESENTED TO MONSEIGNEUR LE PRÉSIDENT DE MESME

I'm glad, when telling tales untold before,
To offer reading for the well-born eye,
And in the high-born hand to be sustained.—HORACE

I SUPPOSE, MONSEIGNEUR, IT will not appear unreasonable that I give the title of a thing unheard of to this discourse—which I present to you with as much affection as your favor and the service which I owe you oblige me to do,—since it is certain that of the almost infinite number of men who have taken pen in hand there has not yet been one, to my knowledge, whose advice a man might follow concerning the choice of books, the means of procuring them, and the arranging of them in the most useful and attractive manner for a handsome and stately library.

For we have, indeed, the counsel which Juan Bautista Cardona, Bishop of Tortosa, gave for the setting up and maintenance of the Royal Library of the Escorial; be it, however, that he has glided over the subject so lightly that no one reckons him of any consequence, at least he should not retard the happy design of those who would undertake on this subject to impart greater light and more explicit directions to others, with the hope that, if they succeed no better than he, the difficulty of the enterprise will excuse them as well as him and exempt them, like him, from all blame and reproach.

Equally true it is, that it is not every man's talent to acquit himself well on this subject, and that the pain and difficulty we undergo in acquiring even a superficial knowledge of all the arts and sciences, in delivering ourselves from the servitude and slavery of certain opinions which make us speak of things and pass upon them capriciously, and in judging discreetly, and without passion, of the merit and quality of authors, are difficulties more than sufficient to persuade us that what Justus Lipsius elegantly (and much to the purpose) said of two other sorts of persons may with equal truth be said of a librarian: "Consuls are made every year, and new proconsuls; but it is not every year that the king or the poet is born."

And if I, Monseigneur, assume the boldness to present you these notes and instructions, it is not that I so much value and esteem my own judgment as to inject it into an affair of so great difficulty, or that I am so far tickled with self-love as to imagine there is that in me which is so rarely to be encountered among others;

ADDRESS TO HIS PATRON

but the warm desire that I have to do something which may be acceptable to you is the only reason that prompts me to combine the opinions common to many learned persons, versed in the knowledge of books, and the several practices of the most famous librarians, with what I could supply from my own limited study and experience, that I may set before you in these counsels the principles and practices which one must follow in order to succeed in this noble and generous enterprise.

Therefore, Monseigneur, after I have made it my most humble request that you would attribute this tedious discourse rather to the candor and sincerity of my affection than to any presumption of being able to acquit myself in it more worthily than another, I shall tell you frankly that unless your designs be to equal the Vatican Library or the Ambrosian of Cardinal Borromeo, you already have wherewith to set your mind at rest and to keep you happy and contented in possessing such a quantity of well-chosen books that though your library be not of the dimensions of those others it is yet more than sufficient not only to serve your own personal enjoyment and the eager interest of your friends but to maintain likewise the reputation of being one of the most considerable and best-provided libraries of France since you have in it all the most important volumes in the principal divisions of learning, and a very great number of others which may be useful for the special and unusual subjects that present themselves from time to time.

But if your ambition be to render your name illustrious by that of your library, and to add this means of achievement to those which on all occasions you employ through the eloquence of your speech, the soundness of your judgment, and the distinction you lend to those high commissions and magistracies which you have so successfully supported, in order to lend an eternal luster to your memory and assure you while you live that you may deliver yourself with ease from the various complications and confusions of ages past, and live exalted in the memories of men, it will be needful to augment, and every day to perfect, what you have so happily begun, and by degrees so to improve your library that it may become as unparalleled as yourself, without equal, and as fair, perfect, and accomplished as it can be made by the industry of man, who never effects anything without some lack and imperfection. "So true it is that nought in every part can win the guerdon of full blessedness."

Why Establish a Library?

NOW, MONSEIGNEUR, since all the difficulty of this design consists in your determining whether it be appropriate for you to undertake it—there being no question of your ability to carry it to completion,—it will first be necessary, before we turn to those precepts which may serve for putting it in execution, to recite and explain the reasons which are most likely to persuade you that it is to your advantage and that you ought by no means to neglect it. For—to come directly to the heart of the matter—common sense tells us that it is altogether laudable, generous, and worthy of a courage which defies mortality, to save from oblivion, preserve, and erect again, like another Pompey, all these images, not of the bodies, but of the minds of so many distinguished gentlemen, who have spared neither time nor industry in transmitting to us a lively portrait of what was most noble in themselves. This project is also one which the younger Pliny, who was by no means the least ambitious of the Romans, would seem particularly to wish to encourage in us by these fine words in his *Epistles,* Book V: "It seems to me a peculiarly noble thing not to permit those who deserve immortality to fall into oblivion." Furthermore, collecting a library, besides being the unusual thing and far from trivial or vulgar, may turn out to be one of those happy tokens of which Cardan speaks in his chapter *De signis eximiae potentiae,* since, being extraordinary, difficult, and of great expense, it cannot but cause everyone to speak well, and with admiration, of him who puts it into effect. "Reputation and report," says the same author, "are rulers of human affairs." Indeed, if we find it not strange that Demetrius made a show and parade of his artillery and his vast and prodigious machines, Alexander the Great of his manner of encamping, the kings of Egypt of their pyramids, nay, even Solomon of his temple, and others of the like—as Tiberius well observes in Tacitus: "Other men shape their policies on the basis of what they think is to their profit. The lot of princes is different; for them, every act should be aimed at glory,"—how much more ought we then to esteem those who have never sought after these superfluous and for the most part unprofitable inventions, wisely judging and believing that there was no means more honorable, nor more sure, of acquiring a great reputation among men than the establishing of fair and magnificent libraries in order to devote them afterward to the use of the

WHY ESTABLISH A LIBRARY? 7

public? It is true also that this enterprise has never misled or deceived those who have known how to manage it well and that it has always been judged of such consequence that not only private persons have benefited by success in it—as Richard de Bury, Bessarion, Vincenzo Pinelli, Sirleto, Henri de Mesme your grandfather of most happy memory, the English knight Bodley, the late Président de Thou, and many others,—but even the most ambitious have always been glad to make use of it to crown and consummate all their glorious achievements, like the keystone of an arch which adds luster and ornament to all the rest of the building. And I need cite, in support of what I say, no other examples than the great kings of Egypt and of Pergamum, Xerxes, Augustus, Lucullus, Charlemagne, Alfonso of Aragon, Matthias Corvinus, and that great prince Francis the First, who have all of them particularly desired and sought (among the almost infinite number of monarchs and potentates who have also resorted to this shrewd device) to amass great numbers of books and to erect fine, well-furnished libraries—not that they were not otherwise entitled to praise and fame, having acquired, on the contrary, more than enough by the triumphs of their great and signal victories, but because they understood that those persons "whose minds and spirits glory alone inflames" should neglect nothing which might easily elevate them to the supreme and sovereign degree of esteem and reputation. And further, should one inquire of Seneca what should be the works of these great and able geniuses who seem to have been sent into the world only to perform miracles, he would without fail answer: "That which is low and mean pleases no man of exalted gifts; the vision of great achievements summons and attracts him." And therefore, Monseigneur, it seems much to the point, since you are preëminent in all important affairs, that you never content yourself with a mediocrity in things which are good and laudable, and further, since there is nothing mean or vulgar about you, that you should also cherish above all others the honor and reputation of possessing the most perfect and the best-furnished and maintained library of your time. Finally, if these arguments cannot dispose you to this enterprise, I feel certain at least that the promise of personal satisfaction will of itself be strong enough to make you resolve upon it; for if it be possible in this world to attain any sovereign good, any perfect and complete contentment, I definitely believe that none is more desirable than the fruitful entertainment and agreeable recreation which a learned man may derive from such a library—a man who is not so much interested in books "for ornaments of dining rooms as for tools of scholarship,"—since because he has a library he may with

WHY ESTABLISH A LIBRARY?

reason call himself cosmopolite, or citizen of the whole world; since with it he may know all, see all, and be ignorant of nothing; since, in short, he is absolute master of this contentment, because he may manage it after his own fancy, enjoy it when he will, quit it when he pleases, maintain it as much as he likes, and—without contradiction, without effort, and without trouble—instruct himself and learn the exactest particulars "of all that is, that was, and that may be, in earth, the farthest heavens, and the sea."

I shall say, then, in summing up all these reasons—and many others which it is easier for you to supply for yourself than for anyone else to set down,—that I do not intend hereby to engage you in any superfluous or extraordinary expense, since I do not subscribe to the opinion of those who consider gold and silver the heart and soul of a library and who persuade themselves (esteeming books only by their cost) that there is nothing good to be had but what is dearly purchased. Neither is it my intention to persuade you that so great a collection can be made without cost or with your purse closed, knowing well that the saying of Plautus is as true in this respect as in many others, "He who seeks gain must make an outlay"; rather would I show you by the present discourse that one may employ many expedients much easier and cheaper, to attain at last the goal which I propose to you.

Preparing for the Task

AMONG THESE EXPEDIENTS, Monseigneur, I consider none more useful and necessary, before plunging into this enterprise, than first to be well instructed oneself concerning the order and the method which should be carefully observed toward accomplishing its end. This may be effected by two easy and sure means. The first is to take the counsel and advice of those who are capable of giving it, of planning, and of animating us *viva voce,* whether they are able to do so because they are men of letters, sober and judicious, who therefore can speak to the purpose, discourse, and reason well upon every subject, or because they also are pursuing the same enterprise with a reputation for better success, and for acting with greater diligence, caution, and judgment than others are doing, such as are at present MM. de Fontenay, Hallé, Du Puy, Ribier, Descordes, and Moreau, in following whose examples one cannot err, since, as Pliny the younger says, "It would be exceedingly stupid not to set oneself the best models"; and, for what concerns you in particular, the variety of their procedures may continually provide you with some new skill and enlightenment which will, perhaps, be serviceable to the progress and advancement of your own library, in the choice of good books and of whatever else is most interesting in each of theirs. The second is to consult, and diligently to collect, the little advice that may be found in the books of some authors who have written however slightly and as a matter of form upon this matter—as for instance the counsel of Bautista Cardona, the *Philobiblon* of Richard de Bury, the Life of Vincenzo Pinelli, Possevino's *De cultura ingeniorum,* what Lipsius has written concerning libraries, and all the several tables, indexes, and catalogues,—and to guide oneself also by the greatest and most famous libraries ever erected, since, to follow the advice and precept of Cardan, "The men most to be believed in any matter are those who have given in themselves the ultimate example of it." After which, one should not fail to have all the catalogues transcribed, not only of the great and most famous libraries—whether ancient or modern, public or private, in this country or abroad,—but also of the small private collections which for not being much known or frequented remain buried in perpetual silence. This will in no way appear strange if one considers the four or five principal reasons which have caused me to advance this proposal. The first, that nothing can be done in imitation of other libraries unless, by means of their catalogues which have been compiled, one knows what they contain. The second, that catalogues can instruct us concerning the books themselves, the place and year of their printing, and their shape and size. The third, that inasmuch as a mind which is generous and nobly born ought to have the desire and ambition to assemble, as in one lot, what others possess as single items, "let those things which, when divided, make people happy, flow together." The fourth, that by this means one may sometimes serve and please a friend, when one cannot provide him the book he requires, by directing him to the place where he may find a copy, as may easily be done with the assistance of these catalogues. Finally, that since it is altogether impossible that we should by our own industry learn and know the qualities of so vast a number of books as a library should have, it is only reasonable to follow the judgment of the most intelligent and best versed, deducing this inference: since these books have been collected and purchased by such and such, there is reason to believe that they deserved it for some circumstance unknown to us. Indeed, I may truly say that in the course of the two or three years that I have had the honor of occasionally meeting with M. de F. at the booksellers I have frequently seen him buy books so old, ill-bound, and wretchedly printed that I could not but smile and at the same time wonder—until, when later he took the trouble to tell me the cause and the circumstances for which he purchased them, his reasons seemed so pertinent that I shall never be convinced that he is not the most learned man in the knowledge of books and that he does not discourse of them with more experience and judgment than any other man, not only in France, but in all the world beside.

The Number of Books

THE FIRST DIFFICULTY having been thus stated and explained, the second, which must follow and engage our close attention, obliges us to inquire next if it be to the purpose to collect a great number of books and to make a library famous, if not by the quality of them, yet at least by the unparalleled and prodigious quantity of its volumes. For, indeed, it is the opinion of many that books are like the laws and opinions of the jurisconsults, which, as one says, "are valued by weight and quality, not by number," and that he alone can discourse suitably upon any point of learning who has least occupied himself with the wide range of reading afforded by those authors who have written upon it. And in truth it seems that those fine precepts and moral reminders of Seneca: "Books enough, yes; but nothing for show. A mass of books burdens but does not aid the learner; better devote oneself to a few authors than ramble about through many. Since you cannot read as many books as you may have, it is enough to have as many as you may read,"—and divers others like them, which he gives us in five or six places in his works, may in some measure favor and strengthen this opinion with the authority of so great a person. But if we wish to upset it in order to establish our own as more probable, we need only rest our case on the great difference that exists between the hard work of any individual whatever and the mere ambition of him who desires to make a show by means of his library, or between him who wishes to satisfy himself alone and him who seeks to oblige and give pleasure to the public. For it is certain that all the foregoing reasons point only to the instruction of those who would judiciously, and with order and method, move ahead in the subject which they pursue, or rather, to the condemnation of those who set themselves up as scholars and pretend to great abilities although they no more view the vast heap of books which they have collected than hunchbacks (to whom King Alfonso was wont to compare them) see those huge humps which they carry behind. This is justly rebuked by Seneca in the passages quoted above, and in yet plainer terms where he asks, "What are countles books to me, and libraries of which the owner in his whole life will scarcely read the titles?"—as also by that epigram which Ausonius with much charm and artlessness addresses to Philomusus:

> That with bought books thy library thou hast fill'd,
> Thinkest thou thyself learn'd, and in grammar skill'd?
> Then, stor'd with strings, lutes, fiddlesticks now bought,
> Tomorrow thou musician may'st be thought.

But with you, Monseigneur, who have the reputation of knowing more than anyone has been able to teach you and who deprive yourself of all sorts of pleasures in order to enjoy and immerse yourself completely in the special delight which you take in courting good authors—with you it properly rests to have one of the most ample and majestic libraries that have ever been erected, so that it may never be said hereafter that it was only for want of a little care, such as you will presently have taken, to bestow this gift upon the public, and upon yourself, that all the actions of your life failed to surpass the most heroic exploits of the most illustrious persons. And therefore I shall always think it very much to the point to collect for this purpose all sorts of books (under such precautions, nevertheless, as I shall later establish), since a library which is erected for public use ought to be general, but can never be so unless it contains all the principal authors who have written upon the great diversity of particular subjects and chiefly upon all the arts and sciences—of which, should one consider the vast number in the *Panepistemon* of Politian, or in another exact catalogue lately compiled, I have no misgivings that anyone will form a judgment, from the great quantity of books which a library ordinarily offers on ten or twelve subjects, of the yet greater number which it would be necessary to have in order to satisfy the curiosity of readers upon all the rest. I do not wonder, therefore, that Ptolemy, king of Egypt, collected for this purpose not one hundred thousand volumes, as Cedrenus would have it; not four hundred thousand, as Seneca reports; not five hundred thousand, as Josephus assures us; but seven hundred thousand, as Aulus Gellius, Ammianus Marcellinus, Sabellicus, and Volaterranus all testify and with one accord; or that Eumenes, the son of Attalus, collected two hundred thousand; Constantine, a hundred and twenty thousand; Sammonicus, tutor to the emperor Gordian the younger, sixty-two thousand; Epaphroditus, merely a professor, thirty thousand; and that Richard de Bury, M. de Thou, and the knight Bodley gathered together so many that the catalogue of any one of their libraries amounts to a volume in itself. It must be said also that there is nothing more to the credit of a library than that every man finds in it what he seeks, having failed to find it elsewhere; since it may be laid down as a maxim that there is no book whatsoever, be it never so bad or disparaged, but may in time be sought for by someone, since, according to the satirist:

> Thousands the types of men; things can be used all ways;
> Each has a will his own; not all one purpose praise.

And since it is commonly with readers as it was with Horace's three guests, "With gullet various seeking food diverse," libraries can be compared to nothing better than to the meadow of Seneca, where every living creature finds that which is most proper for it, "the ox, grass; the hound, the hare; the stork, a lizard." And besides, it must be assumed that every man who seeks for a book judges it to be good and, conceiving it to be so without being able to find it, is forced to esteem it curious and very rare; so that, coming at last upon it in some library, he readily believes that the owner of the library knew it as well as himself and had bought it for the same reason that prompted him to search after it, and thus he conceives an incomparable esteem both for the owner and for the library; which opinion being afterward published, there will be need of but few like experiences, joined to the common opinion of the vulgar, "to whom big things are good," to satisfy and recompense a man who gets little enough honor and glory to justify all his expense and pains. And besides, if one considers times, places, and new inventions, no man of judgment can doubt that it is much easier at present to possess thousands of books than it was for the ancients to get hundreds, and that therefore it would be a shame and eternal reproach to us to be inferior to them in this particular, in which they may be surpassed with such advantage and ease. Finally, as the quality of the books greatly increases the esteem of a library among those who have the means and the leisure to examine it, so one must insist that the mere quantity of them gives it luster and reputation both among foreigners and travelers and among many others who, having neither time nor opportunity to leaf through it interestedly, book by book, may just as easily judge, at a glance, from the prodigious number of its volumes, that there must needs be many which are good, noteworthy, and remarkable. Nevertheless, neither to abandon this infinite quantity without a definition, nor to destroy in those who are interested any hope of being able to carry to completion so fair an enterprise, it seems to me expedient to follow the practice of those physicians who prescribe the quantity of drugs according to their quality, and to state that one cannot be mistaken in collecting all those books which by quality and condition should be placed in a library. To understand which, one must make use of many definitions and precautions, which may more easily be put to use, as chance offers, by those who have a wide acquaintance with books and who make sane and dispassionate judgments on all things, both those which are reduced to writing and there buried, being almost infinite in number, and, to be quite frank about it, some also of those which combat opinions generally held, and maintain paradoxes.

Selecting the Books

I WILL NOW SAY, NOTWITHstanding, in order to omit nothing which may serve us for a guide and beacon in this quest, that the prime rule which one ought to observe is, in the first place, to furnish a library with all the first and principal authors, both ancient and modern, chosen from the best editions (collected works or single books), along with the best and most learned interpreters and commentators that are to be found in every field of learning, not forgetting those that are least common and consequently more interesting—as, for example, the several Bibles, the Fathers and the Councils, for theology at wholesale; Nicholas of Lyra, Hugo, Tostado, Salmerón, for the Positive philosophers; St. Thomas, Occam, Durand, Peter Lombard, Henry of Ghent, Alexander of Hales, Giles of Rome, Albertus Magnus, Aureolus, Burley, Capreolus, Major, Vásquez, Suárez, for the Scholastics; the corpus of civil and canon law; Baldi, Bartolus, Cujas, Alciati, Dumoulin, for jurisprudence; Hippocrates, Galen, Paulus Aegineta, Oribasius, Aëtius, Trallianus, Avicenna, Avenzoar, Fernel, for medicine; Ptolemy, Firmicus, Haly, Cardan, Stöffler, Gaurico, Giuntino, for astrology; Alhazen, Vitellio, Bacon, Aguillon, for optics; Diophantus, Boethius, Jordanus, Tartaglia, Siliceo, Luca di Borgo, Villefranche, for arithmetic; Artemidorus, Albumazar, Synesius, Cardan, for dreams; and so with all the others, which it would be too long and troublesome to specify and enumerate precisely.

In the second place, to procure in their proper languages and particular idioms all the old and new authors that are worthy of consideration—the Bibles and Rabbis in Hebrew; the Fathers in Greek and Latin; Avicenna in Arabic; Boccaccio, Dante, Petrarch in Italian—together with their best translations, Latin, French, or such as are to be found, these latter being for the use of many persons who have not the knowledge of foreign tongues, and the former because it is much to the purpose to have, in their natural channels, without art or disguise, the springs whence so many streams do glide, and further, because ordinarily a more certain clarity and richness of conception are apparent in those which retain and preserve their luster only in their original languages, like paintings in the proper light—not to speak of the necessity also which one may have for the verification of texts and passages ordinarily debated or challenged.

Thirdly, such authors as have best handled the parts of any science or field of learning, whatever it be: as

Bellarmine for controversial theology; Toledo and Navarre, cases of conscience; Vesalius, anatomy; Mattioli, the history of plants; Gesner and Aldrovandi, that of animals; Rondelet and Salviani, that of fishes; Vicomercatus, that of meteors; and the like.

In the fourth place, all those that have best commented upon or explained any author or book in particular: as Pereira upon Genesis; Villalpandi, Ezekiel; Maldonatus, the Gospels; Monlorius and Zabarella, the *Analytics;* Scaliger, Theophrastus' *History of Plants;* Proclus and Marsilio Ficino, upon Plato; Alexander and Themistius, upon Aristotle; Flurance Rivault, Archimedes; Theon and Campanus, Euclid; Cardan, Ptolemy; and so for all sorts of books and tractates, ancient or modern, which have found interpreters and commentators.

Next, all who have written or compiled books or tractates upon any particular subject, general or specific: like Sánchez, who has treated marriage at length; Sainctes and Du Perron on the Eucharist; Gilbert on the lodestone; Maier, the tree-bird; Scortia, Wendelin, and Nogarola, concerning the Nile; and similarly for all sorts of special dissertations on law, divinity, history, medicine, or whatever else it may be, with this reservation nevertheless, that the one which most nearly approaches the profession a man is following be preferred to others.

Moreover, all those who have written most successfully against any science, or who have opposed with most learning and force (without, however, introducing any innovation or any change in principles) the books of some of the most famous and renowned authors. Hence one must not omit Sextus Empiricus, Sánchez, and Agrippa, who say they have upset all the sciences; Pico della Mirandola, who has so learnedly refuted the astrologers; Eugubinus, who has blasted the impiety of the Salmonians and the irreligious; Morisot, who has overthrown the error of the chemists; Scaliger, who has been so successful in opposing Cardan that in some parts of Germany he now has a greater following than Aristotle himself; Casaubon, who dared attack the Annals of that great cardinal, Baronio; Argenterio, who has taken Galen to task; Thomas Erastus, who has so pertinently refuted Paracelsus; Charpentier, who has so vigorously opposed Ramus; and finally, all those who have engaged in like mental fencing and who are so linked together that it were as great an error to read them separately as to hear and judge one party without the other, or one opponent without his antagonist.

Neither may all those who have introduced or modified anything in the sciences be omitted, for it is merely flattering the bondage of man's feeble wit if the scanty knowledge that we possess of these authors is buried under the disdain to which they are inescapably subject for having set themselves up against the ancients and having learnedly examined what others were used to accept as by tradition. For this reason, since of late more than thirty or forty authors of reputation have declared themselves against Aristotle; since Copernicus, Kepler, Galileo, have quite altered astronomy; Paracelsus, Severinus the Dane, Duchesne, and Crollius, medicine; and since many others have introduced new principles and upon them have established strange and unheard-of reasoning, such as had never been foreseen, I affirm that all these authors are requisite to a library, since, according to the common saying, "novelty too is the most pleasant of all things," and—not to linger over so weak a reason—since it is certain that the knowledge of these books is so useful and valuable to him who can consider and draw profit from all that he sees that it provides him a thousand openings and new conceptions, which, being received by a mind that is open, inquiring, and free from prejudice, "bound to no master fealty to swear," make him speak to the purpose on all subjects, deliver him from the admiration which is the true mark of our weakness, and enable him to discourse upon whatsoever presents itself with a great deal more judgment, foresight, and resolution than many persons of letters and merit are used to do.

Furthermore, in the choice of books, one should note whether they be the first that have been composed upon the matter of which they treat, since it is with men's learning as with water, which is never more fair, pure, and limpid than at its source, all invention coming from the first authors, and imitation, with repetitions, from the others: as one sees clearly that Reuchlin, who first wrote of the Hebrew tongue and the Cabbala, Budé of Greek and coins, Bodin of the Republic, Cocles on physiognomy, Peter Lombard and St. Thomas on scholastic theology, have done better than those many others who have engaged themselves in writing about these subjects since their time.

Moreover, one should note whether the subjects of the books are trivial or unusual, interesting or neglected, difficult or easy, since one may well apply to books that are interesting and new what is said of all things that are not commonplace,

Scarce things give pleasure, and therefore we value first-fruits from the orchard;
Such too the reason the rose, winter-grown, fetches a price.

Acknowledging, then, this precept, we should open our libraries to receive, first of all, those who have written on little-known subjects that had not been treated before, in other than a fragmentary and desultory way, as Liceti, who has written *De spontaneo viventium ortu* and *De lucernis antiquorum;* Tagliacozzi, *How to Repair a Slit Nose;* Libavius and Goclenius, on magnetic ointment,—secondly, all worthwhile and less usual books, such as the writings of Cardan, Pomponazzi, Bruno, and all those who have written concerning the Cabbala, mnemonic devices, the Lullian art, the philosopher's stone, divinations, and the like matters. For, though most of them teach only hollow and unprofitable things, and though I hold them but as stumbling blocks to all who amuse themselves with them, nevertheless, to have something with which to please the weaker wits as well as the strong and at the least to satisfy those who desire to see them in order to refute them, one should collect the books on these subjects, although they ought to be considered among the rest of the volumes in the library like serpents and vipers among other living creatures, like tares in good wheat, like thorns among roses—and all this in imitation of the natural world, in which these unprofitable and dangerous things help to round out the masterwork and the scheme by which it was accomplished.

And this maxim should lead us to another of like consequence, which is, not to neglect all the works of the principal heresiarchs or adherents of religions that are new and that differ from the one more commonly revered among ourselves as being more sound and true. For they make a good showing since the earlier among them (to say nothing of the more recent ones) have been chosen from among the most learned men of the last century, who, thanks to I know not what notion and too great love of novelty, quit their cassocks and the banner of the Roman Church to enroll themselves under that of Luther and Calvin, and since those of the present time are not admitted to the exercise of their ministry till after a long and severe examination in the three tongues of the Holy Scripture and the chief points of philosophy and theology,—they make a good showing, I repeat, since, barring disputed passages, they may sometimes score points off the others, as they have done in many nonsignificant treatises, on which they often work with much industry and success. Since it is necessary, therefore, that our scholars should find these authors somewhere available in order to refute them; since M. de T. posed no objections to collecting them; since the early Fathers and Doctors had them at hand; since many of the clergy keep them in their libraries; since there are no scruples about having a Talmud or a Koran, which belch forth against Jesus Christ and our religion a thousand blasphemies infinitely more dangerous than those of the heretics; since God permits us to profit from our enemies—in the words of the Psalmist, "we should be saved from our enemies and from the hand of all that hate us"; since they can be prejudicial only to those who, lacking the basis of right conduct, suffer themselves to be carried away by the first puff of wind that blows, and seek out the shade of a beanstalk, and—to conclude in a word—since the intention which determines all our actions for good or ill is not vicious or hardened, I think it neither an absurdity nor a danger to have in a library (under the restrictions, nevertheless, of license and permission obtained from the responsible authority) all the works of the most learned and famous heretics, such as Luther, Melanchthon, Pomeranus, Bucer, Calvin, Beza, Daneau, Gualther, Hospinian, Paré, Bullinger, Marlorat, Chemnitz, Ochino, Peter Martyr, Illyricus, Osiander, Musculus, the Centuriators, Dujon, Mornay, Dumoulin, and even many others of less consequence "who in the shade of their little fame are buried."

It should also be a rule that all the sets and collections of different authors writing upon the same subject—such as the Talmud, the Councils, the works of the Fathers, *Thesaurus criticus, Scriptores Germanici, Turcici, Hispanici, Gallici, Catalogus testium veritatis, Monarchia imperii, Opus magnum de balneis, Authores gyneciorum, De morbo Neapolitano, Rhetores antiqui, Grammatici veteres, Oratores Graeciae, Flores doctorum, Corpus poetarum*, and all those which contain similar collections— should of necessity be put into libraries, the more since they save us, in the first place, the trouble of searching for a host of books extremely rare and uncommon; and secondly, because they make room for many others and relieve the pressure on a library; thirdly, because they gather together for us in one convenient volume that for which we should otherwise have to search laboriously in many places; and finally, because they are less expensive—as it is certain that it does not require as many pence to purchase them as it does pounds to possess separately all those authors whom they contain.

  I consider it a rule as important as any of the preceding, that one should choose and select, from the plethora of those who have written and who continue daily to write, the authors who appear like eagles among the clouds or like stars sparkling in the dark, those rare geniuses

> from whose abounding lips
> All future time draws for its fields of thought

to whom one may turn as to the most expert masters of every kind of knowledge, and from whose works— not only from all their books, but even from their smallest fragments, occasional papers, and the words of wisdom they have let fall—one may draw, as from a nursery garden of unlimited possibilities, for enriching a library. As it would be absurd to employ the necessary space and money for collecting all the works (and I know not what rubbish) of certain common and contemptible authors, so would it be a patent oversight and inexcusable fault, in those who profess to have all the best books, to neglect any of them, for example those of Erasmus, Ciaconius, Onuphrius, Turnebus, Lipsius, Génébrard, Antonius Augustinus, Casaubon, Salmasius, Bodin, Cardan, Patrizzi, Scaliger, Mercuriale, and others, whose works we have to take with our eyes closed and no choice given, reserving the right of selection in order to escape being deceived about the pedestrian books of authors decidedly inferior; the more since, as one cannot possess too much of that which is good and highly select, so neither can one have too little of that which is bad and from which there is no hope of receiving any obvious profit or use.

Neither may all sorts of commonplace books, dictionaries, miscellanies, books of variant readings, collections of sententious remarks, and other like repertories be overlooked, since these are as so much work done and matter ready prepared for those who have the industry to use them to advantage, it being certain that there are many who work wonders at speaking and writing who have seen scarcely any books besides those mentioned—whence it is, as they commonly say, the Calepino (which serves to describe dictionaries of all sorts) is the livelihood of schoolmasters,—and even if I do say it, of many of the most famous personages as well, it will not be without justification, since one of the most renowned of them had more than fifty books of this sort which he was interminably consulting, and he, having come upon a difficult word on opening the book of Equivokes just as it was handed to him, turned immediately to one of these dictionaries and transcribed out of it, upon the margin of the first book, more than a page of writing, all this in the presence of a mutual friend to whom he could not refrain from saying that those who should see this remark would easily believe that he had spent more than two days in composing it, though he had in truth only the pains of transcribing it. And for my part I consider these collections highly useful and necessary, because the brevity of our life and the multitude of things which we are now obliged to know if we are to be reckoned among the learned do not permit us to do all by ourselves; besides, since it is not granted to every man in every age to have the means of working solely on his own resources, without picking other men's brains, what harm is there in it if those who are industrious enough to imitate nature and so to diversify and appropriate to their own subject what they extract from others, "so that, even if it is obvious from what source it is derived, it may appear nonetheless to be other than its source,"—what harm is there if they borrow from those who seem to have been made for no other purpose than to lend, and draw from pools and stores made for the purpose, since we see that both painters and architects ordinarily create excellent and incomparable works by means of colors and materials which others grind and prepare for them.

Lastly, in this connection, one should put into practice Hippocrates' aphorism which advises us to make concession to time, place, and custom; that is to say, certain kinds of books being sometimes in vogue in one country and not so in another, in the present age though not in the past, it is well to provide more of them than of the others, or at least to have enough of them to testify that we are accommodating ourselves to the times and that we are not ignorant of changes in the popular taste. And hence it is that one frequently finds in the libraries of Rome, Naples, and Florence many works of Positivist theology; in those of Milan and Pavia, many of civil law; in those of Spain and the ancient ones of Cambridge and Oxford in England, much Scholasticism; and in those of France, a good deal of history and polemics. Like differences may also be seen in the varying taste of succeeding centuries, in the ascendancy which in turn the philosophy of Plato, that of Aristotle, the Scholas-

SELECTING THE BOOKS 33

tics, classical letters, and controversial theology have had, each enjoying its period of dominance; just as we see that today the study of morals and politics occupies the attention of most of the best and ablest scholars of this age, while lesser wits amuse themselves with fiction and romances, concerning which I will say only what Symmachus once said of the same kind of literature: "Without substance, captious loquacity is displeasing."

The foregoing ordinarily accepted rules and maxims having been sufficiently explained, there remains in order to finish this chapter on the quality of books nothing but to propose two or three other principles, which will undoubtedly be considered absurd and calculated only to clash with the opinions commonly held and deeply rooted in the minds of many whose esteem for authors is based only on the number and size of their books and who judge their talent and worth only by that for which we customarily despise all other things, namely, their great age and dilapidation, resembling in that respect the opinions of the old man whom Horace depicts in his works as

> given to praise time past,
> A critic of today, tomorrow's judge,

the character of these prepossessed minds being for the most part so smitten with the antique works and ideas that they would not so much as look even from afar upon any book whatever whose author were not older than the mother of Evander or than the forefathers of Carpentras, nor believe that time could be well employed in reading any modern authors, since according to what they say these are but rhapsodists, copyists, or plagiarists, who in no way approach the eloquence, the learning, and the noble conceptions of the ancients, to whom for this reason they cleave as tightly as the polyp to the rock, without departing in the least either from their books or their doctrines, which they never hope to comprehend till they have chewed them over all the days of their lives; it is therefore not extraordinary if, after all their figuring, and when they have sufficiently toiled and sweated, they resemble that ignorant Marcellus who boasted everywhere that he had read Thucydides eight times, or that Nonnus of whom Suidas speaks, who had read his Demosthenes ten times, without ever being able to plead any cause or discourse about anything whatever. And in truth there is nothing more apt to make a man a pedant and banish him from common sense than to despise all modern authors in order to court exclusively a certain few ancients as if they alone were the sure guardians of the highest favors that the wit of man may hope for, or that Nature—jealous of the honor and reputation of her elder sons—should have wished, to our prejudice, to exert her powers to the

SELECTING THE BOOKS 35

utmost that she might heap upon them alone all her graces and liberality. Most certainly, I believe that no one except our friends the antiquarians can hold fast to such opinions or feed upon such fables, since so many new inventions, so many fresh opinions and principles, so many diverse and unthought-of alterations, so many learned books, famous men, new conceptions, and finally so many wonders which every day we see appearing, clearly demonstrate that wits are stronger, more refined, and nimbler than ever before, and that today one may state with perfect assurance that

> The arts have taken upon them in these latter days a new beauty;
> None of them but doth surpass that which erstwhile it hath been,

or make the same judgment of our time that Symmachus made of his: "We have an age friendly to merit in which, if the worthy man does not win himself reputation, it is the fault of the man, not of his generation."

Hence we may conclude that it would be a gross fault in one who professes to collect a library not to place in it Piccolomini, Zabarella, Achillinus, Nifo, Pomponazzi, Liceti, Cremonini, along with the old interpreters of Aristotle; Alciati, Tiraqueau, Cujas, Dumoulin, along with the *Code* and the *Digest;* the

Summa's of Alexander of Hales and of Henry of Ghent, along with that of St. Thomas; Clavius, Maurolico, and Vieta, along with Euclid and Archimedes; Montaigne, Charron, Verulam, along with Seneca and Plutarch; Fernel, Sylvius, Fuchs, Cardan, along with Galen and Avicenna; Erasmus, Casaubon, Scaliger, Salmasius, along with Varro; Commines, Guicciardini, Sleidanus, along with Livy and Cornelius Tacitus; Ariosto, Tasso, Du Bartas, along with Homer and Virgil, and so right down the list with all the most famous and renowned modern authors. Had the capricious Boccalini undertaken to balance modern writers with the ancients, he would perhaps have found a great many of the ancients less able than they and few who surpass them.

The second principle, which will perhaps be no less a paradox than the first, is directly contrary to the opinion of those who value books only by their price and bulk and who are well pleased and think themselves greatly honored to have Tostado in their libraries because he is in fourteen volumes or Salmerón because there are eight, neglecting meanwhile to procure many little books, among which are often found some so well and learnedly composed that there is more profit and pleasure to be found in reading them than in reading many others which for the most part are uncouth, heavy, undigested, and ill-polished

SELECTING THE BOOKS 37

masses; according to Seneca's dictum, "It is difficult not to be foolish among big things," and what Pliny said of one of Cicero's orations, "Tully's longest oration is considered his best," cannot be applied to these monstrous and gigantine books since indeed it is almost impossible that wit should always remain intent upon these great undertakings and that the imagination be not stifled nor the intellect overwhelmed by the mass and chaotic confusion of things to be set down; whereas on the contrary what causes us to appreciate small books which nevertheless treat of serious matters, or deal with some point shown in high relief, is that their authors perfectly command their subjects, as the workman and artist does his material, and that they may better chew, concoct, digest, polish, and mould it according to their fancies than those vast collections of great and prodigious volumes, which for this reason are often but chaos, panspermy, and abysses of confusion,

> mass indigest and rude,
> Nor aught save sluggish weight, and, glomerate,
> Discordant seeds of elements ill-joined.

Hence the unequal success that is to be observed between certain authors, for example between the satires of Persius and of Filelfo, the *Trial of Wits* of Huarte and that of Zara, the arithmetic of Ramus and that of Forcadel, Macchiavelli's *Prince* and that of more than fifty pedants, the logic of Dumoulin and that of Vallius, the Annals of Volusius and the Histories of Sallust, the Manual of Epictetus and the Moral Secrets of Loriot, the works of Fracastoro and those of numberless philosophers and physicians; so true is that which St. Thomas has well spoken, "Nowhere is art more a whole than in the smallest details," and what Cornelius Gallus was wont to promise himself concerning his small elegies,

> Nor for our volumes so few do we gather a less reputation
> Than do the others whose works there's never a library will hold.

But that which most astonishes me in this matter is that such and such a person will neglect the major and minor works of some author while they remain scattered and separated, and afterward burn with a desire to have them when they are collected and bound together in one volume; these persons will neglect, for example, the orations of James Crichton because they are to be found only printed separately, and nevertheless be sure to have in their libraries those of Raymond, Gallutius, Nigronius, Bencius, Perpinián, and many other authors, not that they are better or more fluent and eloquent than those of the learned Scot, but because they are to be found in certain volumes bound up together. Certainly, if all little books should be neglected, there would be no need

SELECTING THE BOOKS 39

of considering the minor works of St. Augustine, Plutarch's *Morals,* the books of Galen, nor of the greatest part of those of Erasmus, of Lipsius, Turnebus, Mizauld, Sylvius, Calcagnini, Franciscus Picus, and many like authors, no more than of thirty or forty minor authors in medicine and philosophy, of the best and most ancient among the Greeks, and of many more among the theologians, because they have all been issued separately, one after another, and in volumes so small that the greatest of them frequently do not exceed in size half a spelling book. Therefore, since one may bind together that which was separate in the printing and join with others what would be lost if alone, and since, in fact, there are many matters which have never been treated except in those little books concerning which it may rightly be said, as Virgil does of bees, "What mighty hearts beat in such tiny breasts," it appears to me altogether fitting that we should take them from bookstalls and old shops, and from any place where they may be found, in order to have them bound with others by the same author or on the same subject and to place them afterward in a library, where I am sure they will win admiration for the industry and diligence of the Aesculapiuses who are so well skilled in joining and reassembling the scattered and separated members of those poor Hippolytuses.

The third, which at first glance may appear to be contrary to the first, opposes in particular the opinion of those who are so intoxicated and infatuated with all new books that they neglect and take no account not only of all the ancients but also of flourishing and renowned authors who were popular six or seven hundred years ago—that is to say, from the time of Boethius, Symmachus, Sidonius, and Cassiodorus to that of Picus, Politian, Barbaro, Gaza, Filelfo, Poggio, and Trapezontius,—such a multitude of philosophers, divines, jurisconsults, physicians, and astrologers as merely by their black and gothic printings disgust our overdelicate students of this age, not suffering them so much as to cast an eye upon them but with a blush and with scorn for those who composed them. This arises from the fact that the ages, or the great spirits who appear in them, have differing talents and inclinations quite unlike, not long maintaining the same tone for any one study or scientific devotion and having nothing so certain as their constant shift and change. Indeed, we see that immediately after the birth of the Christian religion (not to take things back any further) the philosophy of Plato was universally followed in the schools—and most of the Fathers were Platonists,—and that it so continued till Alexander of Aphrodisias elbowed it forcibly aside to make room for that of the Peripatetics and open up a way for the

Greek and Latin interpreters. They were so much engrossed in explaining Aristotle's text that we might still be believing it without much profit, had not the Questionists and Scholastics, led by Abelard, entered the lists in order to predominate everywhere, with the greatest and most universal approbation that was ever given to anything whatsoever, and that, too, for the space of about five or six centuries, after which the Heretics recalled us to the interpretation of the Holy Scriptures and caused us to read the Bible and the holy Fathers, which had continually been neglected amidst these hair-splittings—in pursuit of which the Controversy now stands for all that concerns theology,—and the Questionists along with the Novators, who build upon new principles or else reëstablish those of the ancients, Empedocles, Epicurus, Philolaus, Pythagoras, and Democritus, for philosophy. The other fields of study were not exempt from like changes; in them there is always the generality of spirits who follow these fads and novelties, as surely as a fish does the tide, to the point of worrying no more about what they have once abandoned and of saying rashly, like the poet Calpurnius:

> Cheap in our eyes whate'er in former years
> We saw; what once we gazed on, commonplace.

Thus, the greater number of the good authors are left on the sands, abandoned and neglected by everyone, while our new censors or plagiarists take their places and enrich themselves with their stolen clothes. And in truth it is strange and unreasonable that we should follow and approve, in philosophy for example, the teachings of the University of Coimbra and Suárez and neglect the works of Albertus Magnus, Nifo, Aegidius, Saxonia, Pomponazzi, Achillinus, Herveus, Durandus, Zimara, Buccaferreus, and many of the like, from whom all the great books which we now follow are compiled and transcribed word for word; that we should have an almost unparalleled esteem for Amatus, Driverius, Capivaccio, Montano, Valescus, and almost all the modern physicians, and be ashamed to place in our libraries the books of Hugo Senensis, Jacopo Forli, Jacobus de Partibus, Valescus, Gordon, Thomas Dinus, and all the Avicennists, who have really followed the genius of their age, rude and vulgar in the barbarity of their Latin, but who have yet gone so far into the profundities of medicine, according to Cardan's own confession, that many of our moderns—who have not sufficient resolution, persistence, and assiduity to pursue and imitate—are obliged to lay hands on some of their arguments in order to refurbish them *à la mode* and to make vainglorious show of them, while they themselves dwell only on the tops of the verbal flourishes, where, without going deeper, "They pluck the flowers and reach for the topmost tips." Shall it, then, be said that Scaliger and Cardan, the two greatest figures of the last century, were of one mind in praising Richard Suiseth, otherwise called the Calculator, who lived within these last three hundred years, ranking him among the ten greatest scholars that ever were, without our being able to find his works in any of the most famous libraries? And does it look well that the followers of Occam, prince of the Nominalists, should forever be deprived of seeing his works; or all philosophers, those of the great and renowned Avicenna? It seems, indeed, to be showing small judgment in the choice and knowledge of books to neglect all those authors who should be the more studied the rarer they are and because they will be able from now on to take the place of manuscripts, since there is almost no hope that they will ever be reprinted.

Finally, the fourth and last of these principles concerns only the choice and selection which one ought to make of manuscripts, in order to oppose the practice introduced and generally accepted by reason of the great vogue now enjoyed by the critics who have taught and accustomed us to value higher some manuscripts of Virgil, Suetonius, Persius, Terence, and other ancient authors, than any by those gentlemen who have never been either seen or printed—as if there were any decency in following forever the whims, fancies, or frauds of these modern censors and grammarians who uselessly apply the best years of their lives concocting empty conjectures and begging corrections of the Vatican, in order to alter, correct, or fill in the text of some author who may already have taken up the time of ten or twelve men, although one could readily dispense with them, at need; and it would be most unfortunate, and should be a cause for regret, that the lucubrations and labors of an infinity of great men who have labored and sweated perhaps all their lives long to give us knowledge of something that had never been known before, or to elucidate some profitable and necessary matter, should be lost or should rot away in the hands of some ignorant possessor. Nevertheless, the example of these critics has been such, and their influence so strong, that notwithstanding the dislike which Robortello and certain others of them have inspired in us, even for the manuscripts themselves, yet have they so far bewitched the world into searching for them that they are the only things now in fashion and judged worthy of places in libraries:

> Thus everywhere is mind impoverished;
> Thus slopes to trifles everywhere the road.

Therefore, since it is of the very essence of a library to have a great number of manuscripts—because they are now most in demand and least available,—I sub-

SELECTING THE BOOKS 45

mit, Monseigneur, with reservation for your being better advised, that it would be very desirable for you to continue as you have begun, providing your library with manuscripts that have been composed, neat and complete, upon any worthy subject, like those which you have already had search made for, not only here but at Constantinople, and all that are obtainable of the many authors ancient and modern mentioned by Neander, Cardan, Gesner, and listed in all the catalogues of the best libraries—but not all those copies of books, already in print, which at best can only assist us with some empty and trifling conjectures. It is not my intention, nevertheless, to scorn or to cause this kind of book to be entirely neglected, well knowing by the example of Ptolemy what importance one ought always to attach to copies at first hand or for those two sorts of manuscripts which Robortello (in relation to criticism) prefers to all others.

Lastly, to conclude this chapter on the quality of books, I add what is true both for manuscripts and for printed volumes: not only should one follow the foregoing suggestions and choose accordingly—for instance, if it were a question of Bodin's *République,* to conclude that one should have it because the author was one of the most widely known men of his time and, among the moderns, the first to treat this subject, because the subject is exceedingly necessary and much studied now, and because the book is widely distributed, has been translated into several languages, and reprinted almost every five or six years,—but one should bear in mind the following principle, to wit, to buy a book if the author be good though the matter itself be but common and trivial, or, if the subject of it be difficult and little known, though the author has no reputation, and finally, to follow as occasion demands many other rules which it would be impossible to reduce to an art or method. The foregoing makes me believe that a man may acquit himself worthily of this responsibility if his judgment is not perverted, rash, filled with absurdities, or clouded by puerile opinions, which cause many to despise and reject all that is not to their taste, as if one should govern himself according to the whims of his fancy, or as if it were not the duty of a wise and prudent man to consider all things impartially and never to judge them by the prejudices of others but only by weighing thoughtfully their actual character and usefulness.

Procuring the Books

NOW, MONSEIGNEUR, that I have pointed out in the three preceding chapters what course one ought to pursue to inform oneself on establishing a library, with what quantity of books it should be furnished, and of what quality the books so chosen should be, there follows here a consideration of the means by which they may be procured and how to improve and augment a collection. Upon all which, I shall definitely assert that the first precept which is to be tendered on this subject is to preserve with care those which have been acquired and continue daily to be added, allowing none to be lost or in any manner made away with, "For it is more endurable," says Seneca, "and easier not to acquire things than to lose them, and consequently you will notice that those on whom fortune has never smiled are happier than those whom it has deserted." A library will never be much benefited if that which is collected with so much pains and industry should be lost for want of care; and therefore Ovid and the wisest men had reason to say that it was no less a virtue to preserve a thing than to acquire it. "To keep one's gains equals more gains to seek."

The second is that we neglect nothing which is of any account and which may be of use either to ourselves or others, such as are satires, broadsides, theses, scraps, proofs, and the like, which one should take care to unite and gather according to their types and their subjects (because only thus may they be considered) and so to arrange matters "that what avail not singly, help when joined." Otherwise, it ordinarily happens that for having despised those little books which appear only as trifles and things of no consequence we lose many a rare collection, such as are sometimes the most curious things in the whole library.

The third may be deduced from the means that were employed by Richard de Bury, Bishop of Durham, Lord Chancellor and Lord High Treasurer of England, which consist of publishing and making known to everybody one's affection for books and strong desire to form a library; for this being widely known, it is certain that if he who is pursuing this project has sufficient influence and authority to do favors for his friends, there will not be one among them but will hold it an honor to present him the rarest books that come to hand, who will not admit him freely into his library or into those of his friends, or, in brief, who will not strive to aid this project and contribute to it all that he possibly can; as is well observed by the same Richard de Bury in these very words, which I transcribe the more willingly because his book is rare and of the number of those which are getting lost through our neglect: "When our affairs became prosperous," says he, "on attaining the notice of the King's Majesty, being received into his household, we obtained a larger opportunity of visiting wheresoever we would and of hunting, as it were, through certain very choice preserves, to wit, the private and public libraries, both of the clergy and of laymen"; and a little further on, "There was opened to us through regard for the King's favor a ready entrance for freely searching into the hiding places of books. Indeed, the flying rumor of our love for books now spread everywhere—so much so that we were reported to be even languishing from our desire for them, chiefly for ancient books, and that anyone could easier obtain our favor by quartos than by money. Wherefore, being supported by the authority of the aforesaid Prince, we could notably advance or hinder, promote or obstruct, both the great and the small; and there consequently flowed to us in place of pledges and presents, in place of gifts and prizes, bleared quartos and decrepit tomes, precious alike in our sight and our affection. Then the chests of the noblest monasteries were opened; cases were brought forth, caskets were unlocked, etc." To which he further adds the several voyages which he made as an ambassador, and the great number of learned and interested persons of whose labor and skill he made use in this search. And what yet further induces me to believe that these practices would have some effect is that I know a man who, being interested in medals, pictures, statues, cameos, and other cabinet pieces, has collected by this means alone more than twelve hundred livres' worth without having spent four. Indeed, I take it for a maxim, that every civil and good-natured man will always second the laudable projects of his friends, provided they be not prejudicial to his own. So that he that has books, medals, or paintings which have come to him by chance rather than from any special liking he has for them may easily be persuaded to accommodate among his friends that man whom he knows to be eagerly collecting them. I shall willingly add to this third bit of advice the trickery which magistrates and persons of authority may practice and exercise by means of their dignities; but I would not more nakedly state it than by the simple narration of the strategem which the Venetians made use of in order to obtain the best manuscripts of Pinelli as soon as he was dead. Upon the advice which they had that his library was about to be transported from Padua to Naples, they hastily dispatched one of their magistrates, who seized a hundred bales of books, among

PROCURING THE BOOKS 51

which there were fourteen that contained manuscripts, and two of them more than three hundred commentaries on all the affairs of Italy, alleging for their reasons that, though they had permitted the late Signor Pinelli, out of regard for his position, his purpose, his laudable and irreproachable life, and, principally, for the friendship which he ever manifested toward the Republic, to have their archives and calendars of state papers copied, yet it was neither fit nor expedient for them that such documents should be divulged, laid bare, and communicated after his death. Whereupon his heirs and executors, who were powerful and within their rights, having filed suit against them, these Venetians retained only two hundred of these commentaries, which were placed in a chamber apart, with this inscription: "These things have been removed from the Pinelli Library by order of the Senate."

The fourth is to reduce the superfluous expense which many squander to no purpose upon the binding and ornamentation of their books, in order to employ the savings in purchasing such as are lacking, that thus they may not be objects of that censure of Seneca's, who has a merry jest at the expense of those "to whom the outsides and the name tags of their books give the most pleasure"; and this all the more willingly since binding is nothing but a condition and form of appearance without which—without, at least, one so splendid and sumptuous—books do not cease to be useful, suitable, and rare (only the ignorant esteem a book for its cover), seeing it is not with books as with men, who are known and respected only for their robes and their dress. Thus it is a great deal better and more necessary to have, for example, a large number of books well bound after the ordinary fashion than to have only a little room or case full of volumes cleansed, gilded, ruled, and enriched with all manner of daintiness and superfluous display.

The fifth concerns the buying of them and may be divided into four or five parts according to the several means which may be employed. Among these, I should set down without hesitation as the first, above all others the promptest, the easiest, and the most advantageous, the acquisition of some other entire and undissipated library. I call it prompt because in less than a day's time one may have a goodly number of rare and learned books which could not be brought together again in a lifetime. I call it easy because one is spared both the pains and the time which would otherwise be expended in purchasing them separately. Finally, I call it advantageous because, if the libraries which are bought be good and well chosen, they serve to augment the prestige and reputation of those who are enriched by them. Whence we see that Possevino so much esteems that of the Cardinal de Joyeuse because it was composed of three others, one whereof had belonged to M. Pithou, and that all the most renowned libraries have grown in this manner: as for instance, that of St. Mark's at Venice, by the gift which Cardinal Bessarion made to it of his own; that of the Escorial, by that great collection which Hurtado de Mendoza had brought together; the Ambrosian of Milan, by the ninety bales which were added to it at one time by the shipwreck and ruin of Pinelli's; the library at Leyden, by above two hundred manuscripts in the Oriental languages which Scaliger bequeathed to it in his will; and finally, that of Ascagno Colonna, by that incomparable collection which Cardinal Sirleto bequeathed it. Whence I conjecture, Monseigneur, that yours cannot but one day emerge famous and renowned among the greatest, by reason of that of your father, which is already so widely acclaimed and universally known from the account of it which has been left to posterity by Lacroix, Fauchet, Marcillius, Turnebus, Passerat, Lambinus, and by almost all the scholars of that rank, who have not been unmindful of the pleasure and instruction which they have received from it.

After the preceding, the means which seems to me to approach nearest to this first point is to rummage time and again through all the stalls of the second-hand booksellers and the old stocks and shops for both bound books and those which have been laid aside in sheets for so long that many men of little experience in this kind of search think they could serve only one purpose, lest "the tunny be cloakless or the olive nude"—although we often encounter excellent books among them, and if the expense be well managed, more may be purchased for ten crowns than one can otherwise buy for forty or fifty, if they are picked up in several places piece by piece, provided, nevertheless, one girds himself with care and patience and considers that one cannot say of a library what certain poets said of our city, "The day that it was born, then first 'twas great," since it is impossible so speedily to accomplish a thing whereof Solomon tells us, that "of making books there is no end," and to the finishing whereof, though M. de Thou has labored twenty years, Pinelli fifty, and many others all their lives long, one must not think that they have reached ultimate perfection, since, however much one may wish to do so, no one is ever able actually to complete a library.

But since it is necessary for the growth and augmentation of such a collection to furnish it diligently with all the new books of any merit and consideration that are being printed in all parts of Europe, and since Pinelli and the rest have for this purpose kept in touch

PROCURING THE BOOKS

with a host of friends and dealers in foreign parts, it would be well to do likewise, or at least to select two or three prosperous, discriminating, and experienced booksellers who by their wide information and travels might provide all kinds of recent printings and make diligent search and inquiry for such books as are ordered from catalogues. It is not so necessary to proceed thus for old books, since the surest means of collecting a large number of them cheaply is to seek for them indiscriminately among all the bookstores, where time and chance are in the habit of dispersing and scattering them.

I do not at all infer, from all the good husbandry proposed above, that it is not sometimes necessary to exceed the limits of this economy in order to purchase at extraordinary prices books so rare that only by this means can one tear them from the hands of men who know their worth. But the attitude in which to approach this difficulty is to consider that libraries are neither built nor esteemed but for the service and benefit which one may receive from them, and therefore one should disregard such books and manuscripts as are valuable only for their antiquity, pictures, illuminations, bindings, and other minor considerations—as, for example, the Froissart which certain dealers offered for sale not long since at three hundred crowns; Boccaccio's *De casibus,* which was valued at a hundred; the Missal; Guinart's Bible; Books of Hours, which are often said to be priceless because of their illustrations and vignettes; Livy and other historians, hand-written and illuminated; Chinese and Japanese books, those that are printed on parchment or on tinted paper of extremely fine cotton and with large margins; and several others of the like stuff,—in order to employ the great sums which they cost for volumes more useful in a library than all these we have mentioned, or others like them, which shall never make the passionate collectors of them so much esteemed as was Ptolemy Philadelphus for giving fifteen talents for the works of Euripides; Tarquin, who bought three Sibylline Books at as great a price as would have purchased all nine; Aristotle, who gave threescore and twelve thousand sesterces for the works of Speusippus; Plato, who paid a thousand denarii for those of Philolaus; Bessarion, who bought thirty thousand crowns' worth of Greek books; Hurtado de Mendoza, who procured a shipload of them from the Levant; Pico della Mirandola, who expended seven thousand crowns on Hebrew, Chaldean, and other manuscripts; or that king of France who engaged his gold and silver plate for a copy of a book belonging to the Bibliothèque des Médecins of this city, as is fully attested by the ancient documents and records of their Faculty.

I further add that it would be expedient also to know from the relations and heirs of many gentlemen whether they have not left some manuscripts with which these latter would part, since it frequently happens that the greatest number of them never succeed in getting half their works printed, be it that they are cut off by death or hindered by the expense, the apprehension of censure or criticism, the fear of not having succeeded very well, the indiscretion of what they have written, their own modesty, and like reasons, which have deprived us of many books of Postel, Bodin, Marcillius, Passerat, Maldonatus, and others, whose manuscripts are frequently encountered in certain men's private libraries or in booksellers' shops. In like manner also one ought to know from year to year what papers the most learned professors of the near-by universities are to read to their classes, both public and private, in order to take pains to have copies made and by this simple expedient to obtain a large number of items as good and as worthy of esteem as are many manuscripts which are dearly bought for their age and antiquity, as, for instance, the *Traité des Druides* of M. Marsille, M. Grangier's *Histoire* and *Traité des magistrats français,* M. Belurger's *Géographie,* the sundry writings of MM. Dautruy, Isambert, Seguin, Duval, Dartis, and, in a word, of the most celebrated professors of all France.

Finally, the man with as great an affection for books as Signor Vincenzo Pinelli may also, as he did, visit the shops of those who often buy old paper or parchment to see whether, by accident or otherwise, there may fall into their hands anything that may be worth collecting for a library. And in truth we should be much encouraged in this search by the example of Poggio, who found Quintilian on a pork butcher's counter when he was at the Council of Constance; also by that of Papire Masson, who encountered Agobardus in the shop of a bookbinder who was ready to back his books with it, and by the similar chance which gave us the manuscript of Asconius. Since, nevertheless, this practice is as uncommon as the zeal of those who make use of it, I would sooner leave it to their discretion than prescribe it as a general and necessary rule.

The Building and Its Location

THIS CONSIDERATION OF the place which should be chosen for erecting and establishing a library might well require as long a discourse as any of the preceding, if the suggestions which one might make could be executed with as much facility as those which we have already proposed and expounded above. But since it falls only to those who can construct buildings expressly for this purpose to observe with care, in so doing, all the rules and requirements which architecture dictates, private citizens usually having to be guided, in placing their libraries as little inconveniently as may be, by the different shapes of their dwellings, it would seem superfluous to make any exact prescription; and truth to tell, I believe this to be the only subject which has moved architects to add nothing to what Vitruvius has said thereupon. Nevertheless, in order not to publish these instructions lame and imperfect, I shall set down briefly my opinion on this matter so that each one may make use of it as he can, or as he shall judge it sound and to his liking.

So far as the site and location where one should build or choose a place suitable for a library are concerned, it seems to me that the common saying, "For verse the writer seeks a quiet retreat," would oblige us to choose a part of the house as far removed as possible from hubbub and annoyance, not only what comes from outside but also what is normal to the family and the domestics, by removing it some distance from the streets, the kitchen, the servants' hall, and like places; to situate it, if that be possible, between some spacious court and a pleasant garden, from which it may enjoy good light, a wide and agreeable prospect, and pure air, unpolluted by marshes, sinks, or dunghills, the whole arrangement so well planned and ordered that it is compelled to share nothing unpleasant or obviously inconvenient.

Now, to bring this about with the most pleasure and the least trouble, it will always be best to place it on the middle floors so that the dampness of the ground will not engender mustiness, a kind of rot that develops imperceptibly on books, and so that the garrets and chambers above may keep it from being as susceptible to the inclemency of the weather as are those which, in keeping their roofs low, are all too easily subject to the inconveniences of rain, snow, and excessive heat. If it be not easy to follow the foregoing suggestions, one should at least take care to raise the book rooms by the height of four or five steps—as I have observed in the Ambrosian Library at Milan,—indeed, as high as possible, both for the sake of appearance and for avoiding the inconveniences mentioned above. If, however, the place be damp and ill-situated, matting for the floor will be necessary, and hangings for the walls, and in winter and wet weather the room should be warmed and dried by means of a stove or at least a fireplace, burning only wood that makes little smoke.

It seems to me, nevertheless, that these circumstances and difficulties are nothing to those which are to be taken into account when one pierces walls in order to admit light, since it is equally important that the library be fully illuminated to the farthest corners and that some thought be taken of the nature of the winds prevailing in the neighborhood, which produce effects as different as their several characters and the places through which they pass. Concerning these matters, I say that two things are to be observed: the first, that the windows of the library (after openings have been made on two sides) be not diametrically opposite, except those which give light to a certain table, so that, the light not being dissipated outside, the place will in consequence remain much better illuminated; second, that the principal openings be always toward the east, both because of the early light which the library may receive in the morning and of the winds which blow from that quarter, which, being warm and dry, do wonderfully temper the air, fortify the senses, subtilize the humors, cleanse the mind, preserve a good mood, improve a bad, and, in a word, are very healthful and salubrious; whereas, on the contrary, those which blow from the west are more troublesome and noxious, and the south winds more dangerous than all the rest, because, being hot and moist, they cause things to moulder, thicken the air, nourish worms, engender vermin, foment sicknesses and keep them chronic, disposing us to new ones—whence the aphorism of Hippocrates, "South winds cause deafness, dimness of vision, heaviness of the head, torpor, and are relaxing"—because they fill the head with certain vapors and humidities which cloud the mind, relax the nerves, obstruct the passages, obfuscate the senses, and render us dull and almost unfit for any sort of action. For these reasons, unable to arrange for east winds, one should have recourse to those from the north, which, cold and dry, engender no humidity and fairly well conserve both books and papers.

Arranging the Books

THE SEVENTH POINT, which definitely seems to require treatment after what has preceded, is that of the order and arrangement which books should have in a library; for without it, certainly, our inquiry would be to no purpose and our labor fruitless, since books are put there for no other reason than to be serviceable as need arises. This, however, is impossible unless they be classified and arranged according to subject matter, or in such other fashion as will facilitate their being found at specified places. I affirm, moreover, that without this order and arrangement a collection of books of whatever size, were it fifty thousand volumes, would no more merit the name of a library than an assembly of thirty thousand men the name of an army if they be not billeted in their several quarters under the orders of their officers, or a great heap of stones and building materials the name of a house large or small till they be properly put together to make a finished structure. As we see that nature, "which has neither planned nor completed anything without method," orders, sustains, and preserves in this unique way so great a diversity of things without the use whereof we could not support or preserve the body, so ought we to believe that to sustain the mind it is needful that the objects and things which it makes use of be so arranged that it may always and at pleasure distinguish some things from others, and discriminate among them as it will, without labor, without difficulty, and without confusion. With books, this could never be accomplished if we tried arranging them after a plan of a hundred cases, as Lacroix du Maine proposes toward the conclusion of his *Bibliothèque française,* or after the odd ideas Giulio Camillo presents in the plan for his collection of dramatic works, and much less again, should one employ the triple division which Jean Mabun infers from these words of the Psalmist, "Teach me discipline, goodness, and knowledge," for placing all books under the three classes and principal headings of Morals, Sciences, and Devotion. For just as, if you press the eel too hard, he escapes your hand, as mnemonic systems spoil and pervert the natural memory, and as we frequently fail of accomplishing many affairs by being too circumstantial and overcautious, even so is it certain that it would be extremely difficult for the mind to adjust itself and become accustomed to this arrangement, which seems to have no other purpose than to torture and eternally crucify the memory under the thorns of those frivolous punctilios and chimerical subtleties, so far is it from easing the pressure in any way, or from justifying the dictum of Cicero, "It is, above all, order that gives light to the memory." For this reason, having no more esteem for an order which cannot be followed than for an author who does not wish to be understood, I conceive that arrangement to be always the best which is easiest, least intricate, most natural, most used, and which follows the subjects of theology, medicine, jurisprudence, history, philosophy, mathematics, humanities, and so on, each of which should be classified under subheadings according to their several divisions, which for this purpose ought to be reasonably well understood by the librarian in charge: as, for example, in theology all the Bibles should be placed first, in the order of their languages; next to these the Councils, Synods, Decrees, Canons, and all that concerns the Constitutions of the Church, and the more since they hold the second place of authority among us; after these, the Fathers, Greek and Latin; then the commentators, scholastics, learned men of various schools, and historians; and finally, the heretics. In philosophy, begin with that of Trismegistus as the most ancient, follow with Plato, Aristotle, Ramon Lull, and Ramus, and conclude with the Novators, Telesio, Patrizzi, Campanella, Verulam, Gilbert, Giordano Bruno, Gassendi, Basso, Gomesius, Charpentier, Gorlaeus, who are preëminent among a thousand others; and so proceed with each field of learning, with these precautions, sedulously to be observed: the first, that the most universal and ancient always take precedence; the second, that the interpreters and commentators be placed apart and sorted according to the order of the books which they explain; the third, that the special treatises follow the order and arrangement which their subject matter should occupy among the arts and sciences; the fourth and last, that all books of similar designation and the same subject matter be most precisely classified and set in the places assigned them; since in so doing the memory is so much refreshed that it would be easy to find instantly, even in a library vaster than that of Ptolemy, whatever book one might wish. To effect this with yet more ease and satisfaction, care must be taken that those published works which are too small to be bound as single volumes be assembled and placed only with such as treat the entire like or identical subject, though it is more to the purpose, in any event, to have them bound as single volumes than to cause much confusion in a library by putting them with others on subjects so extravagantly remote that one would never think of looking for them in such company. I know very well that someone will point out to me two fairly noteworthy inconveniences which accompany this arrangement, namely, the difficulty of satisfactorily classifying and assigning a place to certain books of miscellaneous content in any class or principal field of knowledge, and the constant labor which always attends the disturbing of a library when it is necessary to shelve thirty or forty volumes in different places within it. But I reply to the first that there are very few books that are not reducible to some order, especially when one has a great many, and these being once placed, a very slight effort of memory will serve to remind one where he has put them, and that at the worst one has only to select a certain place in which they may be ranged all together. As to the second objection, it is true that one might avoid some trouble by not setting the books too close together, by leaving a little room at the extremities of the shelves or at the place where each field of learning ends; but it would yet, it seems to me, be much more advantageous to choose some place in which to put all such books as may be purchased every six months, at the expiration of which time they should be ranged among the rest, each in its proper place, the more so because they would all be the better for it, being dusted and handled twice a year. And in any case, I believe that this arrangement, which is the most generally employed, will always be considered much better and easier than that of the Ambrosian Library, and of some others, where all the books are stowed pell-mell by volume and number and distinguished only in a catalogue wherein every item is found under the name of its author; an arrangement which, in order to avoid the inconveniences mentioned above, drags after it an Iliad of other woes—for many whereof one may yet prescribe a remedy, by a catalogue faithfully compiled according to subjects and fields of learning subdivided to their smallest categories.

It only remains to mention manuscripts, which cannot be accommodated better or more conveniently than in some quarter of the library—no good purpose being served in separating them from it, since they are the best, the rarest, and most esteemed part of it. To this add that men are easily persuaded, when they do not see them among the rest of the books, that all those chambers where it is said they are locked up are only imaginary and no more than excuses for those not actually possessed. Furthermore, it should be noted that one entire side of the Ambrosian Library is filled with nine thousand manuscripts, which have all been assembled by the care and diligence of Signor Antonio Olgiati; and in that of M. le Président de Thou, one room on the same floor with the rest—and as easily entered—is set aside for this purpose. In prescribing, therefore, the arrangement which should be followed, it must be borne in mind that there are two sorts of manuscripts and that those which are of a sufficient

ARRANGING THE BOOKS

size may be placed on shelves like any other books, with the precaution nevertheless that if there be any of great consequence, or any to which some prohibition attaches, they be placed upon the uppermost shelves without the title showing, that they may be well removed from both hand and eye, so that they be neither known nor handled but at the discretion of him who has charge of them. This same practice should also be followed for the other kind of manuscripts, which consists of commonplace books and loose sheets, which should be gathered into bundles according to their subjects and placed yet higher than the first class, because, being small and requiring but little time to copy, they would daily run the risk of being taken or borrowed if placed where they might be seen and handled by all, as often happens to books which lie upon desks in the old libraries.

This must suffice for this point, on which there is no need to enlarge since, the order of nature (which is always uniform and self-consistent) being incapable of application because of the wide range and diversity of books, there remains only the order of art, which every man usually wishes to establish to suit himself, according as he finds, by his own good sense and judgment, it will best suit his convenience, as much to satisfy himself as from unwillingness to follow the examples and opinions of others.

Ornament and Decoration

I SHOULD WILLINGLY PASS from the foregoing chapter to that with which these instructions ought to close, were I not reminded by what Typotius so truly says, "Without alluring ornament virtue itself is unknown to the world and as good as dead," to say a few words in passing on the outward show and adornment which is requisite to a library, since this bedizening and decoration seems necessary, because, according to another saying of the same author, "All warlike equipment, all public contrivances, and lastly all domestic furniture is designed for show." Indeed, what makes me the more easily excuse the zeal of those who at present seek after this pomp with a great deal of expense and useless cost is that the ancients have therein been more prodigal than we; for if we care to take up, to begin with, their manner of constructing their library buildings: Isidor will tell us that they were all paved with green marble, and their ceilings gilded; Boethius, that the walls were faced with glass and ivory; Seneca, that the presses and desks were of ebony and cedar. If we inquire what rare and exquisite *objets d'art* they put into them, the two Plinys, Suetonius, Martial, and

ORNAMENT AND DECORATION 71

Vopiscus bear witness in all their works that they spared neither gold nor silver to decorate them with portraits, either in painting or sculpture, of all the famous men. And finally, if one would know what was the ornamentation of the books, Seneca has nothing but censure for the unnecessary and immoderate expenses to which they went in having them painted, gilded, illuminated, and bound with every sort of extravagance, prettiness, and superfluity. But that we may derive some instruction from these extravagances, we ought to pick and choose from these extremes what is so far demanded of a library that you cannot in any wise neglect it without stinginess nor exceed it without prodigality.

I say first of all that so far as books go there is no need of spending too much for binding; it is better to save the money that might be spent on bindings in order to have all your volumes with the most generous margins and best print that are to be found; if you wish only to satisfy the visitor's eye, cover with sheepskin, calf, or morocco the backs of such books as you intend to bind, embellish them with gold fillets and a few fleurons, with the names of the authors, for which one should go to the gilder who usually works for the library, as also to the binder to repair backs and scuffed covers, replace headbands, correct any misplaced gatherings, paste in again the maps and illustrations that have come loose, clean the soiled pages, and, altogether, to maintain the good appearance of the library and keep the books in shape.

Nor is there any point in seeking out and amassing in a library all the pieces and fragments of old statues,

> Half Curii, Corvinus short a shoulder,
> Galba, too, minus a nose—and his ears,

since it is enough for us to have good copies carved or cast of those which portray the most famous literary men, so that we may at one and the same time form a judgment of the minds of authors by their books and of their bodily shape and facial expression by means of these pictures and statues, which—joined to the accounts which many have made of their lives—may serve, in my opinion, as a powerful spur to excite a generous and well-born soul to follow in their footsteps and to continue steadfastly in the spirit of some noble enterprise resolved upon, and to follow the established path.

Even less ought one to use gold on his ceilings, ivory and glass on his walls, cedar for shelves, or marble for his floors, since this sort of display is no longer in style, nor to put books on desks, as the fashion once was, but on shelves that cover entire walls; and in place of such gildings and adornings one may substitute mathematical instruments, globes, maps, spheres, paintings, stuffed animals, stones, and

ORNAMENT AND DECORATION

other curiosities as well of art as of nature which may ordinarily be collected from time to time with very little expense.

Finally, it would be an unpardonable oversight if, after a library has been furnished with all things appropriate, it failed to have its shelves hung with some ordinary serge, buckram, or canvas, usually put on with silvered or gilt nails, both to protect the books from dust and to lend a certain special charm to the whole place; also, if it should be unprovided with tables, rugs, chairs, feather dusters, clocks, pens, paper, ink, penknife, sand, a calendar, and other small items and suchlike instruments, which cost so little and are yet so necessary that no shred of excuse can cloak such as fail to provide them.

The Purpose of a Library

NOTHING NOW LACKS to complete these instructions except to grasp their object and chief application: for to suppose that after all this trouble and expense these lights should be hidden under a bushel and so many great minds condemned to everlasting silence and solitude is to understand ill the purpose of a library, which, no more nor less than Nature herself, "is doomed to lose all profit of itself, should it exhibit to solitude things so great, so noteworthy, so subtly formed, so resplendent, so beautiful (and beautiful not in one regard alone); it would, as you know, prefer to be examined, not merely looked at." Therefore I shall tell you, Monseigneur, with as much freedom as I have affection for your service, that in vain does he strive to carry out any of the preceding suggestions or go to any great expense for books who does not intend to devote them to the public use and never to withhold them from the humblest of those who may reap any benefit thereby, so true is the saying of the poet:

> Merit that hides is mean; what doth it serve
> If sunk in darkness, more than unoared craft,
> Or silent lyre, or bow that's never stretched?

And so, among the Romans, it was one of the chief purposes of the wealthiest, or of those who were most interested in the public good, to have many of these libraries set up and afterward to dedicate and bequeath them to the use of all learned men—so many that, according to the calculation of Petrus Victorius, there were twenty-nine in Rome (according to Palladio, thirty-seven), which were such evident indications of the greatness, magnificence, and splendor of the Romans that Panciroli was right in treating as evidence of our carelessness, and in ranking among the memorable items of antiquity which have not descended to our times, this established proof of the material resources of the ancients and of their goodwill toward men of letters, and he was the more justified because at the present time, at least so far as I can learn, it is only at those of the knight Bodley at Oxford, of Cardinal Borromeo at Milan, and of the Augustinian Friars at Rome, that one may enter freely and without difficulty; all the rest, like those of Muret, Fulvius Ursinus, Montalto, the Vatican, the Medicis, Petrus Victorius at Florence, Bessarion at Venice, St. Anthony of Padua, the Jacobins at Boulogne, the Augustinians at Cremona, Cardinal Seripando at Naples, of Federigo, duke of Urbino, of Nunnesius at Barcelona, Ximénes at Complutum, Rantzau at Breitenburg, the Fuggers at Augsburg, and finally, the King's, Saint-Victor, and that of M. de T., at Paris—all of them fair and admirable,—are neither open to everyone nor so easy of access as are the three first mentioned. For to speak only of the Ambrosian of Milan and to show by these very means how it surpasses, both in greatness and magnificence and in obliging the public, many libraries of the Romans, is it not indeed remarkable that anyone may enter at almost any hour he chooses, stay as long as he pleases, see, read, and take notes from such authors as he desires, and have every means and convenience for doing so, either in public or in private—all without any more trouble than to betake himself there at the customary days and hours, seat himself in the chairs placed there for the purpose, and request from the librarian, or from three of his assistants, who are well housed and paid both to care for the library and to serve all those who come there every day to study, the books he wishes to leaf through.

But, to govern public use of the library with courtesy on the one hand and with all necessary precautions on the other, in my opinion, an honorable and learned man, one who knows books, should be selected and given a commensurate salary and the rank and title of Librarian, in accordance with the practice of all the most famous libraries, in which many gentlemen have considered themselves honored by appointment to

THE PURPOSE OF A LIBRARY 77

such a position and have made it in turn more honorable and more to be desired by reason of their great learning and ability, as for example Demetrius Phalereus, Callimachus, Apollonius Alexandrinus, Aristoxenus, and Zenodotus, who once had charge of the library at Alexandria; Varro and Hyginus, who directed the Palatine in Rome; Leidratus and Agobardus, that on the island of Barbe near Lyons under Charlemagne; Petrus Diaconus, that of Monte Cassino; Platina, Eugubinus, and Sirleto, that of the Vatican; Sabellicus, that of Venice; Wolf, of Basel; Gruter, of Heidelberg; Dousa and Paulus Merula, of Leyden, whom the learned Heinsius has succeeded, as, succeeding Budé, Gosselin, and Casaubon, M. Rigault now governs the Bibliothèque Royale, established by Francis the First and much increased by the great industry and diligence which he brings to the task.

Next, the most necessary thing to do is to make two catalogues of all the books contained in the library, in the first of which they should be so carefully listed according to their various subjects and fields of knowledge that one may see at a glance all the available authors on the first subject that strikes his fancy; and in the other they should be faithfully listed alphabetically by authors, first, that duplications may be avoided, and second, that gaps may be detected, and also that persons who from time to time want to read all the works of certain authors in particular may be accommodated. Once the catalogues are established, the service which one can derive from them is in my opinion very considerable, whether you have in mind the particular advantage which the founder and librarian may receive from them or the renown to be acquired by sharing them with everyone. Thus one avoids any resemblance to those avaricious persons who take no pleasure in their wealth, or to that malicious serpent which allowed no one to approach the Garden of the Hesperides and gather its fruits, especially considering that all things must be appraised according to the balance of benefit and use that may be derived from them, and that books, in particular, are like that one of Horace's which he addresses in his *Epistles:*

> The keys and seals the modest love, you hate;
> Hate to be shown to few; praise what all share.

However, since it were unreasonable to desecrate by carelessness that which ought to be managed with judgment, it should first be noted that, since all libraries cannot be open continuously like the Ambrosian, at least all those persons who have occasion to do so should have free access to the librarian in order to obtain right of entry without delay or difficulty; secondly, that those who may be complete strangers, and all others who are interested only in

THE PURPOSE OF A LIBRARY

certain passages, may see, examine, and make extracts from any kind of printed book they may require; thirdly, that well-known persons of distinction be permitted to carry some few ordinary books to their own lodgings, with these precautions, nevertheless: that this loan should not be for more than a fortnight or three weeks at most and that the librarian should be careful to have registered in a book designed for this purpose, and divided alphabetically, whatever is thus lent out to this person and that, together with the date, the size of the volume, and the place and year of its printing, all this to be acknowledged by the borrower's signature and canceled when the book is returned, the day of its return being noted in the margin, so that one may see how long it has been kept and which borrowers deserve, by the diligence and care they display in their treatment of the books, to receive further loans. Assuring you, Monseigneur, that if it shall please you to continue as you have begun and to enlarge your library that it may serve your personal needs in this way, or in any other which you shall judge to be better, you shall receive wide acclaim, an infinitude of thanks, no mean advantages, and, in short, an indescribable satisfaction, as running your eye over the loan book you recognize the courtesies which you have conferred, the gentlemen you have obliged, the persons who will have seen you, the new friends and devoted servants whom you will have acquired—when, in a word, you judge by finger and eye how much glory and reputation your library will have brought you. To improve and enlarge it, I protest I would willingly, and while I live, contribute all that shall in me lie, as I have already been bold enough to demonstrate to you by these instructions. I sincerely hope in time to polish and expand them, so that they will not blush to come out into the open in order to discuss in full a subject not hitherto treated of, publishing under the title of *Bibliotheca Memmiana* what has so long been wished for, a full and detailed account of Letters and of Books: critical study of authors, the names of the best and most necessary to know in each subject, the scourge of plagiarists, the progress of the sciences, the diversity of sects, the revolution in the arts and disciplines, the decline of the Ancients, the several principles of the Novators, and that fine Pyrrhonian system which postulates the ignorance of all men, under the cover of which I do most humbly, Monseigneur, beseech you to excuse my own, and to receive these modest instructions, though coarse and ill-woven, as an earnest of my good-will, and of that which I promise to present you one day with greater pomp and circumstance.

> Thee we have made in marble for the time;
> If pregnant ewe gives increase, thou'lt be gold.

Notes, References, and Index of Persons

In these Notes the sources of Naudé's numerous quotations are given, so far as we have been able to find them, and a few allusions which might be unfamiliar to the reader are explained.—THE EDITORS.

Notes

Page i

The Latin epigram on the half title of this book is not one of Naudé's numerous quotations; it is from the pen of Jean-Cécile Frey, a Swiss scholar and physician whose lectures Naudé attended when a student in Paris. In English it reads:

> To set a book in order, 'tis a task of every day;
> To set in order authors, that gift is yours, Naudé.

The epigram adorns a page introductory to the Latin translation of Naudé's *Avis,* the *Dissertatio de instruenda bibliotheca...e gallico in latinum idioma translata per P.I.L.M.,* which is to be found on pages 73-134 of Johann Andreas Schmid's *De bibliothecis nova accessio collectioni Maderianae adiuncta* (Helmstädt, 1703). The translation, by an unidentified hand—and a none too certain one, if you should ask us,—is one of Schmid's additions to the second edition (1702) of Joachim Johann Mader's *De bibliothecis atque archivis virorum clarissimorum...libelli et commentationes* (Helmstädt, 1666).

Page iii

The design on our title page, of three crescents interlaced, is the same as was used on the spine of De Mesme's own books, between the bands. A crescent was included in De Mesme's coat of arms.

NOTES

Page 1

"I'm glad, when telling tales...," Horace, *Epistles*, I, 19, 33–34.

The counsel which Cardona gave. The reference is to his *De regia S. Laurentii del Escorial, bibliotheca libellus, sive concilium cogendi omnis generis utiles libros et per idoneos ministros fructuose callideque custodienda* (Tarragona, 1587).

Page 2

"Consuls are made...," Floridus, "De qualitate vitae," in Justus Lipsius, *Electa*, 1, 5.

Page 4

"So true it is...," Horace, *Odes*, II, 16, 27–28.

Page 6

"It seems to me...," Pliny the younger, *Epistles*, V, 8, 1.

"Reputation and report...," Cardan, *De utilitate ex adversitate capienda*, 3, 25 ("De signis eximiae potentiae et gloriae").

"Other men shape their policies...," Tacitus, *Annals*, IV, 40, 1.

Page 7

"whose minds and spirits...," Valerius Flaccus, *Argonautica*, 1, 76–77.

Page 8

"That which is low...," paraphrased from Seneca, *Epistulae morales*, 39, 2.

NOTES

"for ornaments...," paraphrased from Seneca, *De tranquillitate animi*, 9, 5 (Dial. 9, 9, 5).

Page 9

"of all that is...," Liturgy, combined with Virgil, *Georgics*, 4, 222.

"He who seeks gain...," Plautus, *Asinaria*, 217 (I, iii, 65).

Page 10

"It would be exceedingly stupid...," paraphrased from Pliny, *Epistles*, I, 5, 13.

Page 11

"The men...," slightly varied from Cardan, *De util.*, 3, 4 ("De contemptu").

Page 12

"let those things which...," Claudian, *In primum consulatum Stilichonis*, 1, 33–35.

Page 14

"are valued by weight...," inspired by a note of Gaius on coinage in his *Institutiones juris civilis*, 1, 122.

"Books enough, yes...," paraphrased from Seneca, *Tranq.*, 9, 5 (Dial. 9, 9, 5), and *Ep. Mor.*, 2, 3.

Page 15

Hunchbacks. Although Naudé attaches his anecdote to a King Alfonso, Brantôme (*Les Vies des grands capitaines étrangers,* lib. I, ch. xxxii: M. le maréchal de Strozze) tells the same story of Louis XI, who, he relates, "said of a prelate of his realm who had a fine library and never looked at it, that he was like a hunchback who had a fine big hump on his back which he never laid eyes on."

"What are countless books...," Seneca, *Tranq.,* 9, 4 (Dial. 9, 9, 4).

"That with bought books thy library...," Ausonius, *Epigrammata,* 44.

Page 17

"Thousands the types...," Persius, 5, 52.

"With gullet various...," Horace, *Epist.,* II, 2, 62.

Page 18

"the ox...," Seneca, *Ep. Mor.,* 108, 29.

"to whom big things are good," paraphrased from Seneca, *Ep. Mor.,* 118, 7.

Page 21

Dreams. In Naudé's time, philosophical explanations of dreams were still legitimately attempted by learned men.

Page 22

Maier's work on the tree-bird (i.e., the fabled tree-goose or barnacle-goose, believed to be produced from a tree, in the form of a barnacle) is the *Tractatus de volucri arborea, absque patre et matre in insules Orcadum, forma anserculorum proveniente seu de ortu miraculoso...vegetabilium...* (Frankfurt, 1619).

NOTES

Page 23

The Salmonians. In Virgil's inferno (*Aeneid*, 6, 585–594) Salmoneus is depicted as suffering eternal punishment for having attempted a cheap imitation of the attributes and powers of the true Lord of the World, viz., Jupiter; hence, a prototype of antigod, or arch-heretic. Agostino Steuco, an Italian churchman called Steuchus Eugubinus, wrote against heretics, notably his *Pro religione christiana adversus Luteranos* (Bologna, 1530).

Page 24

"novelty too...," Ovid, *Epistulae ex Ponto*, III, 4, 51.
"bound to no master...," Horace, *Epist.*, I, 1, 14.

Page 25

The Republic. Both a subject and the name of a work, Jean Bodin's treatise on government, *De la république* (Paris, 1576). Bodin favored a limited monarchy.
"Scarce things...," Martial, IV, 29, 3–4.

Page 26

The Lullian art. The Catalonian philosopher and mystic, Ramon Lull (*ca.* 1235–1315), wrote, among other works, an *Ars major*, an *Ars generalis*, and an *Ars veritatis inventiva*, which last is probably the work referred to. The Lullian art itself was an attempt at a universal art of discovery.

Page 27

"we should be saved...," Luke, 1: 71.

Page 28

Heretics. Evelyn, in his translation, omitted the names of the heretics although he included the rest of the passage.

The Centuriators. In 1559 there appeared the first volume of a work entitled *Ecclesiastica historia...secundum singulas centurias...per aliquot studiosos et pios viros in urbe Magdeburgicâ*. This was the work of a group of Lutheran scholars who have since been known as the Centuriators of Magdeburg from the manner in which they divided the work (century by century) and the city in which the first few volumes were published.

"who in the shade...," Virgil, *Aeneid*, 5, 302.

Collections: Naudé's insistence on the desirability of collections may not be generally understood today. He was referring to the many Renaissance sets containing all the important works pertaining to a particular subject. The works of Latin grammarians, of writers on agriculture or military science, and many other special categories of books were then available in collections. The brief titles listed by Naudé as examples indicate the following:

Thesaurus criticus. Janus Gruterus, *Lampas, sive fax artium liberalium, hoc est, thesaurus criticus...*, 7 vols., Frankfurt, 1603-1634.

Scriptores Germanici. Marquardus Freher, *Rerum Germanicarum scriptores*, 3 vols., Frankfurt, 1600-1611.

Turcici. Philip Lonicer, *Chronicorum Turcicorum libri III*, Frankfurt, 1578.

Hispanici. Robert Bel, *Rerum Hispanicarum scriptores aliquot*, 3 vols., Frankfurt, 1579.

Gallici. Petrus Pithoeus, *Annalium et historiae Francorum ab anno 708 ad annum 990, scriptores coaetanei XII,* Paris, 1588, and *Historiae Francorum ab anno 900 ad annum 1285 scriptores veteres XI,* Frankfurt, 1596. These were superseded by André Duchesne, *Historiae Francorum scriptores coaetanei ab ipsius gentis origine,* 5 vols., Paris, 1636–1649.

Catalogus testium veritatis. Illyricus (Matthias Flach), Basel [1556]. It is interesting to note that Naudé includes this heretical work.

Monarchia imperii. Melchior Goldast ab Haiminsfeld, *Monarchia s. Romani imperii, sive tractatus de iurisdictione imperiali seu regia, et pontificia seu sacerdotali,* 3 vols., Hanau, 1612, Frankfurt, 1614, 1613, respectively.

Opus magnum de balneis. De balneis omnia quae extant apud Grecos, Latines et Arabas, Venice, 1553.

Authores gyneciorum. Gynaeciorum, hoc est, de mulierum tam aliis tam gravidarum, parientium et puerperarum affectibus et morbis, libri veterum ac recentiorum aliquot, Basel, 1566.

De morbo Neapolitano. Aloysius Luisinus, *De morbo Gallico omnia quae extant apud omnes medicos,* 2 vols., Venice, 1566–1567.

Rhetores antiqui. Rhetores Graeci, 2 vols., Venice, 1508–1509.

Grammatici veteres. Probably, George Fabricius, *Grammaticorum veterum libelli,* Leipzig, 1569.

Oratores Graeciae. Probably, *Oratorum veterum orationes,* Paris, 1575.

Flores doctorum. Thomas Palmer (Thomas de Hibernia), *Manipulus florum* [later entitled *Flores omnium pene doctorum*], Piacenza, 1483.

Corpus poetarum. Pierre de la Brosse, *Corpus omnium poetarum veterum Latinorum*, Lyons, 1603.

Page 29

"from whose...," not identified. The Latin reads:

> ... quorumque ex ore profuso,
> Omnis posteritas latices in dogmata ducit.

Page 30

The Calepino. Ambrosio Calepino (1435–1510), of Calepio in Italy, was the author of a famous Latin dictionary (1502), the first, in the modern sense; whence a calepin (Eng.) is any dictionary or chief book of reference, and a *calepin* (Fr.) a notebook or memorandum book.

Page 31

Book of Equivokes. The reference is probably to the *De aequivocis* attributed to Xenophon but actually written by Joannes Annius Viterbensis. In Naudé's time it was available, for example, in the *Historia antiqua ... Xenophon de aequivocis ...* (Heidelberg, 1599) edited by Judas Bonutius.

"so that, even...," Seneca, *Ep. Mor.*, 84, 5.

Page 32

Hippocrates' aphorism advising men to make concession to time, place, and custom. The idea is expressed in his *Aphorisms*, 1, 2, and *In the Surgery*, 2.

NOTES

Page 33

"Without substance...," Symmachus, *Epistles,* 10, 51.

"given to praise...," slightly varied from Horace, *Ars poetica,* 173-174.

Page 34

Older than the mother of Evander, or than the forefathers of Carpentras. Evander, in the *Aeneid,* is a very old man; and Carpentras is a very old French town. Only an antiquarian interest would rove back to Evander's mother, or to the forebears of Carpentras's oldest inhabitants.

Rhapsodists. A name applied to bards in ancient Greece who stitched together poems already in circulation in order to produce a continuous whole, apparently new.

Page 35

"The arts have taken...," not identified. The Latin reads:

> Sumpserunt artes hac tempestate decorem,
> Nullaque non melior quam prius ipsa fuit.

"We have an age...," paraphrased from Symmachus, *Epist.,* 3, 43.

The *Code* and the *Digest.* That is, Justinian's.

Page 37

"It is difficult...," paraphrased from Seneca, *Naturales quaestiones,* VI, 29, 1.

"Tully's longest...," slightly varied from Pliny, *Epist.,* I, 20, 4.

"mass indigest...," Ovid, *Metamorphoses,* 1, 7-9.

Page 38

Annals of Volusius. A long poem known only by Catullus's scornful reference to it (36, 1); here mentioned in contrast to the scholarly histories of Sallust.

"Nowhere is art..." Although Naudé himself attributes this saying to Thomas Aquinas, it is not to be found in the concordance to the *Summa Theologica* which has been compiled by Professor Roy J. Deferrari of the Catholic University of America; so we are advised by kindness of the compiler. Possibly it is to be found elsewhere in the works of the scholastic philosopher.

"Nor for our volumes...," Anon., "De Cornelio Celso." See Peter Baumann II, *Anthologia veterum Latinorum epigrammatum et poëmatum* (2 vols.; Amsterdam, 1759), Vol. I, bk. II, ep. cclii.

Page 39

"What mighty hearts...," Vergil, *Georgics,* 4, 83.

Page 41

The Questionists. "Habitual or professed questioners, *spec.* in theological matters. In early use applied to certain of the schoolmen, as Aquinas and Duns Scotus." O.E.D.

The Novators. Men who were writing against orthodox Aristotelian philosophy.

"Cheap in our eyes...," Calpurnius Siculus, *Eclogues,* 7, 45–46.

Page 42

The teachings of the University of Coimbra. Late sixteenth- and early seventeenth-century commentaries on

Aristotle by the Jesuits of the University of Coimbra, Portugal.

"They pluck the flowers...," not identified. Sainte-Beuve suggests that Naudé made this up. The Latin reads:

> Decerpunt flores, et summa cacumina captant.

Morhof, in his *Polyhistor* (I, 1, ii, 17), quoting Naudé, prints it as prose, merely ending the sentence.

Page 44

"Thus everywhere...," Palingenius, *Zodiacus vitae,* 3 ("Gemini") (Rotterdam ed., 1698, p. 30).

Page 47

"For it is...," paraphrased from Seneca, *Tranq.,* 8, 2 (Dial. 9, 8, 2).

"To keep one's gains...," Ovid, *Ars amatoria,* 2, 13.

Page 48

"that what avail...," paraphrased from Ovid, *Remedia amoris,* 420.

Page 49

"When our affairs...," Richard de Bury, *Philobiblon,* ch. viii.

King. That is, Edward III.

Page 51

"to whom the outsides...," paraphrased from Seneca, *Tranq.,* 9, 6 (Dial. 9, 9, 6).

Page 53

A lively pen picture of Naudé buying books in Italy, "rummaging through the stalls," as he himself advises, is drawn by Gian Vittorio Rossi in his *Erythraei epistulae* (Cologne, 1645–1649), Vol. II, pp. 18–19. "You might suppose," he says, "that not just one man's devotion but some kind of disaster had swept through all the booksellers' shops. Having bought up in every last one of them all the books, whether in manuscript or in print, dealing in any language whatever with any subject or division of learning no matter what, he has left the stores stripped and bare. Sometimes, moreover, as if he had come to those shops not as a purchaser of books, but to get at the size of the walls, he measures with a surveyor's rod all the books and the shelves clear to the roof, and names his figure on the basis of that measurement. Not infrequently he comes to a place where there are on view heaps of books, piles of a hundred or a thousand apiece; he asks the price; the seller names it; they fail to agree; they wrangle; but in the end it is he who by insisting, by pushing, by beating, and finally by sheer malignancy, has his way so that he carries off the very best volumes cheaper than if they were pears or lemons, while the merchant, thinking over the transaction at his leisure, complains that a cataract was cast over his eyes and his hand forced, because for those books he could have got a far better price from the spice merchants, for casing incense or pepper; or from the food merchants, for wrapping up butter, or fish in sauce and other pickled articles. But you just ought to see the fellow dashing out of the bookshops;

I'm sure you couldn't restrain your laughter; he comes out so completely covered—head, beard, and clothing—with spiderwebs and the dust of learning which had been clinging to the books, that it doesn't seem as if any amount of clothes-shaking or whisking with a brush would suffice to rid him of it."

Page 54

"the tunny be cloakless...," Martial, XIII, 1, 1.

"The day that it was born..." Although Naudé here ascribes this line to poets who have praised Paris, in his *Addition à l'histoire de Louis XI* (1630) he commends Coster for having used it apropos of printing.

Solomon: "Of making books there is no end," Ecclesiastes, 12:12.

Page 56

The Missal. Richly illuminated missals were treasures then, as they are now. A famous one (now MS Harl. 2891), which Naudé may have had in mind, was for a time in the collections of the first Duke of Berry (*fl.* late 14th cent.).

Guinart's Bible. The Bible mentioned here as a very costly acquisition, for the price of which one might enrich one's library with many good books, was perhaps a manuscript copy of *Les Livres historiaux de la Bible,* a late thirteenth-century version by Guiart des Moulins of Peter Comestor's twelfth-century *Scholastica historia;* for example, like that described in the *Catalogue des livres de feu M. le duc de la Vallière* as a "très beau et précieux document sur velin du XIV° siècle," or the better known but less than supreme example called the Poitiers Bible (now in the British Museum), which the English captured with its owner, the French king John II, at the battle of Poitiers. This explanation assumes a misprint of "Guinart" for Guiart; but even the Bibliothèque Nationale, on appeal, suggests no other solution to the problem. For the importance and popularity of Guiart's *Bible historiale,* as it was commonly called, see Samuel Berger, *La Bible française au moyen âge* (Paris, 1884), pp. 156 ff.

King of France. That is, Louis XI, who in 1471 borrowed from the library of the Faculty of Medicine a work in two small manuscript volumes called "totum continens Rhasis," the writings of Rhazes the Arabian physician, to have a copy made for his own library. The Faculty weighed its risk in lending one of its treasures to the king and required him to put up a staggering amount of surety. The borrowed book was duly returned. The story is told in Naudé's *Addition à l'histoire de Louis XI* (1630); also, e.g., in the *Eloge historique de la Faculté de médecine de Paris* (1774), and in Alfred Franklin's *Anciennes Bibliothèques de Paris,* Vol. II (1870), pp. 22 f.

Page 57

The *Traité des Druides* of M. Marsille. Perhaps the M. Marsille mentioned here is an unintended repetition of the Marsille mentioned a few lines earlier. That one, since he is named in company with Postel and Passerat, is quite certainly Théodore Marcile (1548–1617), a famous professor who held the chair of Latin Eloquence in the Collège

Royal de France from 1602 until his death. But the editors of the present book do not find that he ever wrote on the Druids. A likely candidate for the authorship of the *Traité* mentioned is Jean-Cécile Frey (Lat., Janus Caecilius), a Swiss who taught philosophy in the Collège de Montaigu and died of the plague in 1631. His *Philosophia Druidarum,* 1625, is included in the list of his works given by Niceron (*Mémoires,* Vol. 39, pp. 52 f.), and is judged perhaps the most likely to keep his memory green (Larousse, *Dictionnaire...du XIX° siècle*).

Dautruy, Isambert, Seguin, Duval, Dartis. These five learned men, famous in their time, are now so far forgotten that their names are hardly to be found in the biographical dictionaries. Jean Dautruy (d. 1646), whose last will and testament (1642) has been printed in the *Bulletin de la Société de l'histoire de Paris* (47° année [1920]; Paris, 1922), taught sacred literature at the Sorbonne and is said to have written industriously for some thirty-five years. Nicolas Isambert (d. 1642), also of the Sorbonne, taught theology, and wrote numerous theological treatises and a commentary on the *Summa* of Thomas Aquinas. Pierre Seguin (d. 1648) held the chair of medicine at the Collège Royal de France from 1594 to 1630, except for a few years when he relinquished it in favor of his son Michel (d. 1622). After his wife's death, we are told, being out of sympathy with the times and perhaps even more with the court, at which he had official appointments, he retired and took holy orders. It is remarkable that his nephew Claude Seguin just about paralleled his career. Guillaume Duval

(d. 1646) taught philosophy at the Collège for many years. He was a physician besides. (Sketches of these medical men are to be found in Moréri, *Grand Dict. hist.* [nouv. ed.; Paris, 1759], and in the *Notice des hommes les plus célèbres de la Faculté de médecine en l'Université de Paris* [Paris, 1778], edited by Jacques-Albert Hazon.) Guillaume Duval's cousin André (d. 1638), a theologian and zealous defender of orthodoxy, became dean of the faculty of theology at the Sorbonne. Jean Dartis (d. 1651) was professor of canon law at the Collège Royal de France from 1623 until his death.

Page 60

"For verse the writer seeks...," Ovid, *Tristia,* I, 1, 41.

Page 62

"South winds...," Hippocrates, *Aphorisms,* 3, 5.

Page 63

Arranging the books. For serious and not so serious remarks on the problem of arranging books in a library, one should not omit to see the *Quarterly Review,* Vol. LXXII (1843), review of catalogues, etc., pp. 1 ff.; Frantz Funck-Brentano, "Les Problèmes bibliographiques et leur solutions," *Revue des deux mondes,* Vol. CLV (1898), pp. 175-199; and Odell Shepard, essay entitled "Shelving Systems," in *The Art of Forgetting* (Boston, 1929), pp. 230-244.

"which has neither planned...," paraphrased from Aristotle, *Politics,* 1256b 21, and *Physics,* 252a 11 ff. The editors of the present volume are indebted to Professor

NOTES 99

Harold F. Cherniss, of the Institute for Advanced Studies, Princeton, for tracing this reference.

Page 64

The triple division which Jean Mabun infers. Who Jean Mabun may have been, and in what work of his the mention of the triple division first appears, are questions awaiting answer. Morhof, in his *Polyhistor* (Tom. I, lib. 1, cap. v, sect. 3), repeats the dictum, ascribing it to "Johannes quidam Mabunus...cujus mentionem facit Naudaeus." Brunet, in the Introduction to Vol. VI of his *Manuel de librairie,* also repeats it and gives Naudé as his reference. (The spelling "Mabrun" in Brunet's text is presumably a misprint.) It has been suggested, on a mere similarity of names, that the person meant is a late fifteenth-century pietist, Jean de Bruxelles, or Mauburnus, of whom there is notice in the *Thesaurus anecdotorum* of Martène and Durand (5 vols.; Paris, 1717), Vol. III, col. 1302, and in *Gallia christiana*...(16 vols.; Paris, 1716 et seqq.), Vol. VII, cols. 836–837. His name is found elsewhere in various forms, including Momboir.

"Teach me...," paraphrased from the Vulgate, II Chronicles, 1:10. The speaker is Solomon, not David.

Page 65

"It is, above all...," Cicero, *De oratore,* II, 86, 353.

Page 70

"Without alluring ornament...," Typotius, *De fama;* not seen.

"All warlike...," *ibid.*

Page 72

"Half Curii...," Juvenal, *Satires*, 8, 4-5.

Page 73

Among the necessaries for a library, Naudé includes, between the feather dusters and the clocks, *boules jaspées* and *conserves*, which have defied the efforts of translators. Evelyn writes "balls of jasper" and "conserves," without explanation. The unknown author of the Latin translation is hardly more helpful with his "globos vitreos coloratos" (the notion that the *boules* are of glass is apparently his own gratuitous contribution) and his "fructus conditos, quos medici vocant conservos" (pots of jam, or even medicated comfits, hardly seem appropriate to a library table). A possible meaning for *conserves,* for Naudé's as for later times, is some kind of sight-conservers, perhaps reading glasses to ease the strain of conning difficult manuscripts. As for *boules jaspées,* the editors of the present translation do not find the phrase in the dictionaries. Can these objects have been spherical paperweights flattened at the base and pleasantly colored, perhaps like those of our grandfathers' day which had a rose or a spiral of gold inside or at least a "marbled" surface?

Page 74

"is doomed to lose...," paraphrased from Seneca, *De otio,* 5, 3-4 (Dial. 8, 5, 3-4).

"Merit that hides...," Claudian, *De quarto consolatu Honorii,* 222-224.

NOTES

Page 75

Montalto. That is, Pope Sixtus V, who, before becoming a cardinal in 1570, had assumed the name Montalto from an eminence near his native town of Grottamara, in Ancona. He built in Rome the Villa Montalto, which he filled with works of art and books. One of his acts as Pope was ordering the reconstruction of the Vatican Library.

Page 76

The King. Louis XIII, whose reign (1610–1643) included the greater part of Naudé's lifetime.

Saint-Victor. The library of the abbey of Saint-Victor, in Paris, was renowned for its collection of theological works. It is amusing to take a side glance at Rabelais's satirical list (lib. I, ch. vii) of books that Pantagruel found there.

Page 78

"The keys and seals...," Horace, *Epistles*, I, 20, 3–4.

Page 80

The Pyrrhonian system. The followers of Pyrrho of Elis (*ca.* 350–270 B.C.) held that only when men are convinced that they can know nothing may they attain happiness.

"Thee we have made...," Virgil, *Eclogues*, 7, 35–36.

References

(For information about Gabriel Naudé the reader is referred to the following books and articles, especially.)

Anon. "Libraries of Great Men, I: Mazarin," *Book-Lore: A Magazine Devoted to Old-Time Literature*, I (1884–1885): 148–151, 175–177.

Courtney, J. W. "Gabriel Naudé, M.D., Preeminent Savant, Bibliophile, Philanthropist," *Annals of Medical History*, VI (1924): 303–311.

Crawford and Balcarres, Earl of. "Gabriel Naudé and John Evelyn, with Some Notes on the Mazarinades," *The Library: A Quarterly Review of Bibliography*, 4th ser., XII (1932): 381–408.

Franklin, Alfred. "Collège Mazarin," in his *Les Anciennes Bibliothèques de Paris* (3 vols.; Paris, 1867–1873), Vol. III, pp. 37–160; and "Bibliothèque du Roi," *ibid.*, Vol. II, esp. pp. 196–197.

——— "Gabriel Naudé," *Le Bibliophile français*, IV, n° 6 (avril 1870): 321–327, with portrait.

——— "Remise de la bibliothèque de monseigneur le cardinal Mazarin par le sieur Naudé entre les mains de M. Tubeuf," *ibid.*, III, n° 4 (août 1869): 214–219.

Garnett, Richard. *Essays in Librarianship and Bibliography* (London, 1899), pp. 166–168.

Irailh, Augustin-Simon. "Gabriel Naudé, avec les bénédictins," in his *Querelles littéraires, ou mémoires pour servir à l'histoire des révolutions de la république des lettres* (4 vols.; Paris, 1761), Vol. IV, pp. 203–210.

Jacob, le R. P. Louis, ed. *V. cl. Gabrielis Naudaei tumulus... huic accessit catalogus omnium operum ejusdem Naudaei* (Paris, 1659).

Kaulek, Jean. "Documents relatifs à la vente de la bibliothèque du cardinal de Mazarin pendant la Fronde, janvier-février 1652," *Bulletin de la Société de l'histoire de Paris et de l'Ile-de-France,* 8ᵉ année (Paris, 1880), pp. 131–145.

——— "Nouveaux documents pour servir à l'histoire de la bibliothèque du cardinal Mazarin, 1642–1652," *ibid.,* 9ᵉ année (1882), pp. 81–90.

Labitte, Charles. "Ecrivains précurseurs du siècle de Louis XIV, I: Gabriel Naudé," *Revue des deux mondes,* 4ᵉ sér., VII (1836): 447–477.

Moréri, Louis. *Grand Dictionnaire historique,* nouv. éd. (10 vols.; Paris, 1759), art. "Naudé, Gabriel," Vol. VII, pp. 944–945.

Niceron, Jean-Pierre. "Gabriel Naudé," in his *Mémoires pour servir à l'histoire des hommes illustres dans la république des lettres* (43 vols.; Paris, 1729–1745), Vol. IX, pp. 76–110.

Quarterly Review, Vol. CLV (1883), in a review of books relating to Cardinal Mazarin, pp. 87–89.

Rice, James V. *Gabriel Naudé, 1600–1653.* Johns Hopkins Studies in Romance Literatures and Languages, Vol. XXXV (1939).

Rossi, Gian Vittorio. *Iani Nicii Erythraei* [pseud.] *epistolae ad Tyrrhenum* (2 vols.; Cologne, 1645–1649), Vol. I, pp. 4, 119, 128, 130, 153; Vol. II, pp. 16–19, 27–28, 76, 110.

Sainte-Beuve, C. A. "Ecrivains critiques et moralistes de la France: Gabriel Naudé," *Revue des deux mondes,* nouv. ser., 13ᵉ année, IV (1843): 754–789; reprinted in his *Portraits littéraires* (1862), Vol. II, pp. 467–512.

Smith, George. "Gabriel Naudé, a Librarian of the Seventeenth Century," *Library Association Record,* I (1899): 423–431, 483–493.

Index of Persons

Abelard, 41
Achillinus (Alessandro Achillini), 35, 42
Aegidius. *See* Giles of Rome
Aëtius, 20
Agobardus (St. Agobard), 58, 77
Agrippa, Cornelius, 23
Aguillon, François, 21
Albertus Magnus, 20, 42
Albumazar, 21
Alciati, Andrea, 20, 35
Aldrovandi, Ulisse, 22
Alexander, king of Macedon, 6
Alexander of Aphrodisias, 22, 40
Alexander of Hales, 20, 36
Alfonso V, king of Aragon, 7
Alhazen, 21
Amatus Lusitanus, 42
Ammianus Marcellinus, 17
Apollonius of Rhodes, 77
Archimedes, 22, 36
Argenterio, Giovanni, 23
Ariosto, 36
Aristotle, 22, 23, 24, 32, 35, 41, 56, 65
Aristoxenus, 77
Artemidorus Daldianus, 21
Asconius Pedianus, 58
Attalus I, king of Pergamum, 17
Augustine, St., 39
Augustinus, Antonius (Antonio Agustín), 30
Augustus, 7
Aureolus (Pierre d'Auriol), 20
Ausonius, 15
Avenzoar, 20
Avicenna, 20, 21, 36, 43
Azpilcueta, Martín, the "Doctor of Navarre," 22

Bacon, Francis, 36, 65
Bacon, Roger, 21
Baldi de Ubaldis, Pietro, 20
Barbaro, Ermolao, 40
Baronius (Cesare Baronio), cardinal, 23
Bartolus (of Sassoferrato), 20
Basso, Sebastiano, 65
Bellarmine (Roberto Bellarmino), cardinal, 22
Belurger, Claude, 57
Bencius (Ugo Benci), 38, 42
Bessarion, John, cardinal, 7, 53, 56, 75
Beza (Théodore Bèze), 28
Boccaccio, 21, 55
Boccalini, Traiano, 36
Bodin, Jean, 25, 30, 45, 57
Bodley, Thomas, 7, 17, 75
Boethius, 21, 40, 70
Borromeo, Federigo, cardinal, 3, 75
Bruno, Giordano, 26, 65
Buccaferreus (Luigi Boccadiferro), 42
Bucer, Martin, 28
Budé, Guillaume, 25, 77
Bullinger, Heinrich, 28
Burley, Walter, 20

Calcagnini, Celio, 39
Callimachus, 77
Calpurnius, 41
Calvin, 27, 28
Camillo, Giulio, 64
Campanella, Tommaso, 65
Campanus (Giovanni Campano), 22
Capivaccio, Geronimo, 42
Capreolus (Jean Capréole), 20
Cardan, 6, 11, 20, 21, 22, 23, 30, 36, 42, 43, 45
Cardona, Juan Bautista, 1, 11
Casaubon, 23, 30, 36, 77
Cassiodorus, 40
Cedrenus, Georgius, 17
Charlemagne, 7, 77
Charpentier, Jacques, 23, 65
Charron, Pierre, 36
Chemnitz, Martin, 28
Ciaconus (Pedro Chacón), 30
Cicero, 37, 65
Clavius, Christoph, 36
Cocles (Bartolommeo della Rocca), 25
Colonna, Ascagno, cardinal, 53
Commines, 36
Constantine, 17
Copernicus, 24
Cornelius Gallus, 38
Cremonini, Cesare, 35
Crichton, James, 38
Crollius (Oswald Croll), 24
Cujas, Jacques, 20, 35

Daneau, Lambert, 28
Dante, 21
Dartis, Jean, 57

Dautruy, Jean, 57
De Bury, Richard, bishop of Durham, 7, 11, 17, 48–50
Demetrius I, king of Macedon, 6
Demetrius Phalereus, 77
Democritus, 41
Demosthenes, 34
Descordes, Jean, 10
Dinus, Thomas (Tommaso del Garbo), 42
Diophantus of Alexandria, 21
Dousa (Jan van der Does), 77
Driverius (Jérémie Drivère), 42
Du Bartas (Guillaume de Salluste), 36
Duchesne, Joseph, 24
Dujon, François, 28
Dumoulin, Charles, 20, 35
Dumoulin, Pierre, 28, 38
Du Perron, Jacques-Davy, cardinal, 22
Du Puy, Pierre, 10
Durandus (Guillaume Durand), 20, 42
Duval, Guillaume, 57

Empedocles, 41
Epaphroditus, 17
Epictetus, 38
Epicurus, 41
Erasmus, 30, 36, 39
Erastus, Thomas, 23
Euclid, 22, 36
Eugubinus (Agostino Steucho), 23, 77
Eumenes II, king of Pergamum, 17
Euripides, 56

INDEX

Fauchet, Claude, 53
Federigo, duke of Urbino, 75
Fernel, Jean, 20, 36
Ficino, Marsilio, 22
Filelfo, Francesco, 37, 40
Firmicus Maternus, 20
Flurance Rivault, David de, 22
Fontenay, M. de (François du Val, marquis de Fontenay-Mareuil), 10, 12
Forcadel, Pierre, 37
Forli (Jacopo della Torre), 42
Fracastoro, Girolamo, 38
Francis I, king of France, 7, 77
Froissart, 55
Fuchs, Leonhard, 36
Fugger family, 75

Galen, 20, 23, 36, 39
Galileo, 24
Gallutius (Tarquinio Gallucci), 28
Gassendi, 65
Gaurico, Luca, 20
Gaza, Theodore, 40
Gellius, Aulus, 17
Génébrard, Gilbert, 30
Gesner, Conrad von, 22, 45
Gilbert, William, 22, 65
Giles of Rome (Egidio Colonna), 20, 42
Giuntino, Francesco, 20
Goclenius (Rudolf Goeckel), 26
Gomesius (Gometius of Lisbon), 65
Gordian II, Roman emperor, 17
Gordon, Bernard, 42
Gorlaeus, Abraham, 65
Gosselin, Jean, 77

Grangier, Jean, 57
Gruter, Jan, 77
Gualther (Balthasar Walther), 28
Guicciardini, Francesco, 36

Hallé, Pierre, 10
Haly (Ali ibn Rodhwân), 20
Heinsius, Daniel, 77
Henry of Ghent, 20, 36
Hermes Trismegistus, 65
Herveus (Noël Hervé), 42
Hippocrates, 20, 32, 62
Homer, 36
Horace, 1, 4, 17, 33, 78
Hospinian, Rudolf, 28
Huarte (Juan de Díos), 37
Hugo (Hugh of St. Victor), 20
Hugo Senensis. See Bencius
Hurtado de Mendoza, Diego, 53, 56
Hyginus, 77

Illyricus (Matthias Flach), 28
Isambert, Nicolas, 57
Isidor of Seville, 70

Jacobus de Partibus (Jacques Desparts), 42
Jordanus Nemorarius, 21
Josephus, Flavius, 17
Joyeuse, François de, cardinal, 53

Kepler, 24

Lacroix du Maine (François Grudé), 53, 64
Lambinus, Dionysius (Denis Lambin), 53

Leidratus Noricus, 77
Libavius (Andreas Libau), 26
Liceti, Fortunio, 25, 35
Lipsius, Justus, 2, 11, 30, 39
Livy, 36, 56
Loriot, François, 38
Luca di Borgo (Luca Pacioli), 21
Lucullus, 7
Lull, Ramon, 38, 65
Luther, 27, 28

Macchiavelli, 37
Maier, Michael, 22
Major, Johannes (John Mayr), 20
Maldonatus (Juan Maldonado), 22, 57
Marcillius (Théodore Marcile), 53, 57
Marlorat, Augustin, 28
Martial, 70
Masson, Jean Papire, 58
Matthias Corvinus, king of Hungary, 7
Mattioli, Pietro Andrea, 22
Maurolico, Francesco, 36
Medici family, 75
Melanchthon, 28
Mercuriale, Girolamo, 30
Merula, Paulus, 77
Mesme, Henri de (grandfather of Naudé's patron), 7
Mesme, Jean-Jacques de (father of Naudé's patron), 53
Mizauld, Antoine, 39
Monlorius (Juan Bautista Moullor), 22
Montaigne, 36
Montalto (Pope Sixtus V), 75

Montano, Giambattista, 42
Moreau, René, 10
Morisot, Jean, 23
Mornay, Philippe de (commonly known as Duplessis-Mornay), 28
Muret, Marc-Antoine, 75
Musculus (Andreas Meusel), 28

Navarre. *See* Azpilcueta
Neander, Michael, 45
Nicholas of Lyra, 20
Nifo, Agostino, 35, 42
Nigronius (Giulio Nigrone), 38
Nogarola, Luigi, 22
Nunnesius (Hernán Núñez de Guzmán), 75

Occam (William of), 20, 43
Ochino, Bernardino, 28
Olgiati, Antonio, 68
Onuphrius (Onufrio Panvinio), 30
Oribasius, 20
Orsinus, Fulvius (Fulvio Orsini), 75
Osiander, Andreas, 28
Ovid, 47

Palladio, Andrea, 75
Panciroli, Guido, 75
Paracelsus, 23, 24
Paré, Ambroise, 28
Passerat, Jean, 53, 57
Patrizzi, Francesco, 30, 65
Paulus Aegineta, 20
Pereira, Bento, 22
Perpinián, Pedro Juan, 38
Persius, 37, 43
Peter Lombard, 20, 25

INDEX

Peter Martyr (Pietro Vermigli), 28
Petrarch, 21
Petrus Diaconus, 77
Philolaus, 41, 56
Philomusus, 15
Piccolomini, Alessandro, 35
Pico della Mirandola, Giovanni, 23, 40, 56
Pico della Mirandola, Giovanni Francesco, 39
Picus. *See just above*
Pinelli, Gian Vincenzo, 7, 11, 50–51, 53, 54, 58
Pithou, Pierre, 53
Platina (Bartolommeo de Sacchi), 77
Plato, 22, 32, 40, 56, 65
Plautus, 9
Pliny the elder, 70
Pliny the younger, 5, 10, 37, 70
Plutarch, 36, 39
Poggio Bracciolini, Giovanni Francesco, 40, 58
Politian (Angelo Ambrogini), 16, 40
Pomeranus (Johann Bugenhagen), 28
Pompey, 5
Pomponazzi, Pietro, 26, 35, 42
Possevino, Antonio, 11, 52
Postel, Guillaume, 57
Proclus, 22
Ptolemy, 20, 22
Ptolemy Philadelphus, king of Egypt, 17, 45, 56, 66
Pythagoras, 41

Quintilian, 58

Ramus (Pierre la Ramée), 23, 37, 65
Rantzau, Heinrich, 75
Raymond. *See* Lull
Reuchlin, Johann, 25
Ribier, Guillaume, 10
Rigault, Nicolas, 77
Robortello, Francesco, 44, 45
Rondelet, Guillaume, 22

Sabellicus (Marcantonio Coccio), 17, 77
Sainctes, Claude de, 22
Sallust, 38
Salmasius (Claude de Saumaise), 30, 36
Salmerón, Alfonso, 20, 36
Salviani, Ippolito, 22
Sammonicus, 17
Sánchez, Francisco, 23
Sánchez, Tomás, 22
Saxonia (Albert of Saxony), 42
Scaliger, Joseph Justus, 53
Scaliger, J. C., 22, 23, 30, 36, 43
Scortia (Giovanni Baptista Scorza), 22
Seguin, Pierre, 57
Seneca, 8, 14, 15, 17, 18, 36, 37, 47, 51, 70, 71
Seripando, Girolamo, cardinal, 75
Severinus, Petrus, 24
Sextus Empiricus, 23
Sidonius Apollinaris, 40
Siliceo (Juan Martínez Guijarro), cardinal, 21
Sirleto, Guglielmo, cardinal, 7, 53, 77
Sleidanus (Johann Sleidan), 36

Solomon, 6, 54
Speusippus, 56
Stöffler, Johann, 20
Suárez, Francisco, 20, 42
Suetonius, 43, 70
Suidas, 34
Suiseth (Richard Swineshead), 43
Sylvius (Jacques Dubois), 36, 39
Symmachus, 33, 35, 40
Synesius, 21

Tacitus, 6, 36
Tagliacozzi, Gasparo, 26
Tarquin (Tarquinus Priscus), 56
Tartaglia, 21
Tasso, 36
Telesio, Bernardino, 65
Terence, 43
Themistius, 22
Theon of Alexandria, 22
Theophrastus, 22
Thomas Aquinas, 20, 25, 36, 38
Thou, Jacques-Auguste de, 7, 17, 27, 54, 68, 76
Thucydides, 34
Tiberius, 6
Tiraqueau, André, 35
Toledo, Francisco de, cardinal, 22
Tostado, Alfonso, 20, 36
Trallianus (Alexander of Tralles), 20
Trapezontius (George of Trebizond), 40
Turnebus (Adrien Turnèbe), 30, 39, 53
Typotius (Jacques Typot), 70

Ursinus, Fulvius (Fulvio Orsini), 75

Valescus (Valasco de Taranta), 42
Vallius (Paolo Valli), 38
Varro, 36, 77
Vásquez, Gabriel, 20
Verulam. *See* Bacon, Francis
Vesalius, 22
Vicomercatus (Francesco Vimercati), 22
Victorius, Petrus (Pietro Vettori), 75
Vieta, 36
Villalpandi, Juan Bautista, 22
Villefranche (Estienne de La Roche), 21
Virgil, 36, 39, 43
Vitellio (Erasmus Witelo), 21
Vitruvius, 59
Volaterranus (Raffaello Maffei), 17
Volusius, an annalist mocked by Catullus, 38
Vopiscus, Flavius, 71

Wendelin, Marcus Friedrich, 22
Wolf, Hieronymus, 77

Xerxes, 7
Ximénes de Cisneros, Francisco, cardinal, 75

Zabarella, Giacomo, 22, 35
Zara, Antonio, 37
Zenodotus of Ephesus, 77
Zimara, Marco Antonio, 42

www.ingramcontent.com/pod-product-compliance
Lightning Source LLC
Chambersburg PA
CBHW021714230426
43668CB00008B/828